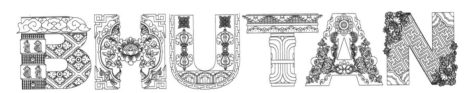

Travelog

Published by Druk Asia Publishing
November 2022
ISBN 978-981-18-1355-9
©Druk Asia

To reach out to the publisher, email **hello@bhutantravelog.com**.

The resources in this book have been provided for informational purposes only. Although the authors have made every effort and taken reasonable care in preparing the book, we cannot warrant the accuracy, adequacy or completeness of the content, and disclaim all liability arising from the use of any of the information.

Front cover image by Scott A. Woodward
Book design by Steve Lim Seng Hee
Edited by Lee Chow Ping
Illustrations by Defry
Photography by Andrew Chun, Ashley Chen, Bhupen Ghimiray, Derek Low, Dorji Dradhul, Inez Bratahalim, Joni Herison, Karma Dorji, Kencho Wangdi, Lester V. Ledesma, Sathya Parthasarathi, Scott A. Woodward, Stephen Gollan, Tian Chad, Tom White, Ugyen Dema, Wiris William, Zahariz Khuzaimah, Bumdeling Wildlife Sanctuary, Royal Office for Media and Tourism Council of Bhutan.

Acknowledgements

Our heartfelt appreciation to the many individuals who have helped make this book possible. First and foremost, we would like to extend our deepest gratitude to the honourable Prime Minister of Bhutan, Dasho Dr Lotay Tshering for taking his time to pen his sincere thoughts for the readers while he was in the quarantine facility.

Special thanks to those who gave their time to share their Bhutan experiences, including Lester V. Ledesma, Karen Lim, Scott A. Woodward, Josephine, the Chan family, Tian Chad, Dato Darren and Datin Kate, Robin Yap, and Baki Zainal. Their personal experiences added tremendous value to the book.

We are immensely grateful to the many talented photographers who have journeyed with us and contributed their beautiful photographs towards the book including Andrew Chun, Bhupen Ghimiray, Derek Low, Dorji Dhradhul, Inez Bratahalim, Karma Dorji, Kencho Wangdi, Lester V. Ledesma, Sathya Parthasarathi, Scott A. Woodward, Stephen Gollan, Tian Chad, Tom White, Ugyen Dema, Wiris William, and Zahariz Khuzaimah.

We are very grateful to our illustrator, Defry, for all the lovely illustrations. Thank you very much to our editor, Chow Ping, for her insightful feedback, comments and suggestions. Our utmost gratitude to our designer, Steve Lim, for his hard work and dedication throughout the creative process.

We greatly appreciate Dasho Kinley Dorji and Pek Sioksian for helping us to proofread and edit parts of the book. Their experience and valuable insights have been extremely enriching for us.

We would also like to thank all our friends in Bhutan including Damcho Rinzin and the Tourism Council of Bhutan who have provided support and encouragement throughout the years. Your friendship and generosity propelled us to continue sharing the beauty of the kingdom with the world.

Last but not least, thank you for picking up this book and supporting our humble efforts in showing you a glimpse of this enchanting country called Bhutan, a special place that is very close to our hearts.

Foreword by the Prime Minister of Bhutan

The request to be a part of this book came my way as I remain comfortably hedged in a room for almost a week now. I am undergoing the 21-day mandatory quarantine at a local hotel in Thimphu, upon return to the country from an official trip.

The state-sponsored quarantine is one of the critical measures to trace and treat COVID-19 cases that have swamped the world in an unprecedented way.

Remaining indoors for three weeks at a stretch contrasts my routine of engaging in duties almost round the clock, a habit I picked up from my two decades as a surgeon.

Easier said than done, but the experience also comes with a dividend to divert some thoughts inward. Therefore, I take this opportunity to share my thoughts from the quarantine facility.

I look around and see that it is a beautiful structure built with aspirations to harbour guests who come to Bhutan for varying reasons. But the pandemic turned the tide and changed the face of tourism altogether. It forced all of us to stay put, shelve our travel plans and let our curiosities rest for a while.

Hotels such as the one I am putting up in are either closed or converted into units to trace, treat or isolate COVID-19 cases.

It also means that now is the time to redefine tourism. For one, our visionary monarchs always believed that tourism in Bhutan should be about discovering and enriching experiences that are exclusive and fundamental in life. It should be about "value" and not "volume".

This wisdom gets reiterated around this time when uncertainties rock the tourism sector across the world. It is time to slow down and contemplate on what one seeks in life. **And this is when your destination matters.**

In this, Bhutan might have the answers. Our kings pioneered the concept of Gross National Happiness, which insists on a unique development framework, a mindful endeavour of securing collective happiness as a nation. Regardless of how we pursue modern development, we are anchored on important pillars that define humanity. Which is why Bhutan will never look at tourism through the lens of money-making. It will not be a destination for 'tourists'. Instead, it will be a place for travellers to experience and find meaning. If you prefer trees to towering buildings, or if you wish to sip water from a flowing river and not plastic bottles, maybe you could consider Bhutan.

Our strength is the leadership we have in His Majesty the King. The unity under the benevolent leader is our fortitude to endure all hardships. With this pandemic, too, His Majesty is spearheading the battle.

The stories of hardship and sacrifices to protect the country and the people will resound for generations.

Confined in this room, my thoughts wander, and I get reminded of a comment a foreign journalist made, "*The world would be a different place if all countries had a His Majesty each. This makes Bhutan all the more special.*"

As I write this note, the region reels under stronger waves of COVID-19. Bhutan is safe and secured for now, but the battle is far from over. We also know that like all crises, we will emerge more percipient. We will have more stories to tell, more experiences to share.

As we do so, we will be happy to offer what you don't find in other parts of the world: **simplicity** and **contentment.** Because this is what Bhutan is about. We will always ensure that the essence of inner peace remains non-compromised and preserved for our next generation as we seek economic development.

Finally, I congratulate Ashley Chen and Joni Herison for putting together this travelogue, which sketches a great view of Bhutan through the colours and features. Through this publication, I hope my thoughts find you with more courage to see through this pandemic, and I pray that we emerge from this stronger and as better human beings.

Dasho Dr Lotay Tshering
Prime Minister
Royal Government of Bhutan

For now, if you ever seek to find answers to some of the fundamental questions in life, please know that there is a country somewhere in the Himalayas that could offer you the answers.

Discover the Magic of Bhutan

"Oh! You are going to Bhutan! Isn't that the happiest country in the world?" a question often posed at the mention of the Kingdom of Bhutan. Until recently, Bhutan has been relatively unknown. In many minds, it is a mystical secluded place. Nonetheless, thanks to the publicity on social media, more and more people are learning about this enigmatic country for its unique philosophy of development that focuses on happiness, vibrant spiritual presence, and its pristine natural environment. Bhutan is also gaining popularity as a travel destination, owing to the credits of international media features and Bhutan's skilful management of the COVID-19 pandemic.

Over the past fifty years, Bhutan has gradually emerged from centuries-long self-isolation to meet modernisation demands. It has been careful with its choices and decisions on the road of development and progression. While Bhutan has opened its doors to the world, a 'High value, Low volume' tourism policy still guides the country to ensure that its unique culture, identity and natural environment will continue to be protected from external influence. In the past, all visitors were required to book their trip to Bhutan through a licensed tour operator.

On Jun 2022, Bhutan passed a new Tourism Levy Bill that marked a new era of tourism in Bhutan. With the adoption of the Tourism Levy Act of Bhutan 2022, the 'Minimum Daily Package Rate' was abolished, and tourists are no longer required to book their trips to Bhutan through any tour operator.

Bhutan Travelog aims to provide you with insights into the country's history, values, customs, as well as travel tips and recommendations. This book also includes 9 exclusive first-hand stories from diverse travellers who have been to Bhutan to provide you with a glimpse into this idyllic country. We hope that their journeys will spark your curiosity and inspire your own journey to this breathtaking kingdom.

Special Feature

The stunning photo on the book cover was beautifully captured by Scott A. Woodward, a Canada-born, Singapore-based highly distinguished photographer. His unique and sensitive photographic style has resulted in him being honoured by Luerzer's Archive as one of the "200 Best Advertising Photographers Worldwide" twice. Nikon also named him "One of Asia's Finest Photographers".

His photographs are featured regularly in a wide variety of publications including *National Geographic Magazine, Condé Nast Traveller, Travel + Leisure, Monocle, Esquire, Vogue, GQ, The Washington Post, The Financial Times* and *The New York Times*.

Keep a lookout for these icons!

The icons are here to help you navigate your reading.

Tips

Tips are important information for tourists who are new to Bhutan. These are things that you should take note of when you're planning a trip to Bhutan.

Ancient Fortresses

This icon represents the great majestic dzong (ancient fortresses) of Bhutan. Each district has at least one dzong that serves as the district monastic body and government administrative centre.

General Sightseeing

These places are for general sightseeing. It's where you get your camera ready for action. Even if you are not a shutterbug, you can simply relax and drink in the stunning landscapes and architecture of the sites.

Activities (Booking required)

If you come across a calendar icon, note that there are activities available on-site. Prior booking is often required. Remember to get in touch with the operators to make arrangements in advance.

Religious Sites

When you see the stupa icon, it means that the place is a sacred site. It can either be a nunnery, a temple, or a place with great religious significance.

Myths and Legends

Bhutan is a country steeped in mythology and folktales. The mystical dragon icon means that the particular site has intriguing myths or legends associated with it. Be sure to delve deeper into it with your tour guide when you are in Bhutan.

Bridges

Due to the mountainous terrains, Bhutanese rely on either suspension bridges or traditional cantilever bridges to get across the crystal-clear rivers. In fact, suspension bridges in Europe were influenced by the iron chain bridges in Bhutan, built by Thangthong Gyalpo.

Festivals

Festivals are very significant in Bhutanese culture. The dancer icon means that the site is a venue for certain festivals in Bhutan. However, the festival dates vary from year to year. For updated information on festival dates, check out **www.bhutantravelog.com.**

Arts and Crafts

There are 13 traditional zorig chusum (arts and crafts) in Bhutan, categorised during the reign of the fourth secular ruler, Tenzin Rabgye. These arts and crafts are integral to Bhutanese culture. The flower icon indicates that the location is popular for Bhutanese traditional arts and crafts.

Proverbs

Bhutanese are generally witty and you're bound to find nuggets of wisdom from the locals that you interact with. Their sense of humour is evident from their fun road signs. Thus, to spice up your reading, we have also inserted some interesting Bhutanese proverbs through the pages.

Proverb

འཇིག་རྟེན་མ་ཕྱིས་དམ་ཆོས་མ་ཧ།

Jig ten ma chi; dam choe ma ha.

Do not start your worldly life too late; do not start your religious life too early.

Contents

About
Bhutan

The first part of the book features the important symbols, history, and governance system of Bhutan. It serves as a glimpse into the kingdom and provides basic understanding of the foundation on which the nation has been built upon.

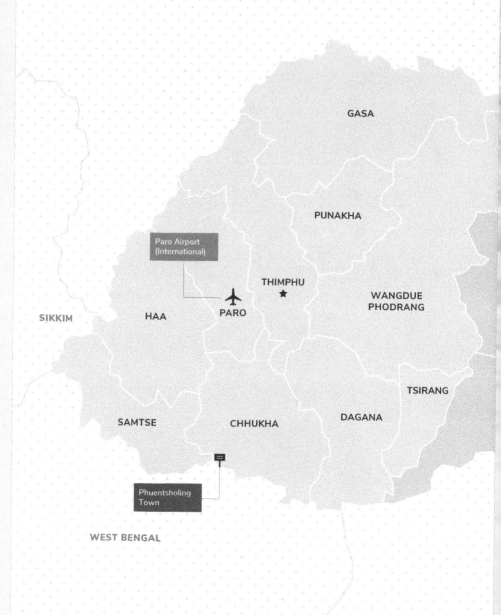

Map of Bhutan

GASA

PUNAKHA

Paro Airport
(International)

THIMPHU
★

WANGDUE
PHODRANG

SIKKIM

HAA

PARO

SAMTSE

CHHUKHA

DAGANA

TSIRANG

Phuentsholing
Town

WEST BENGAL

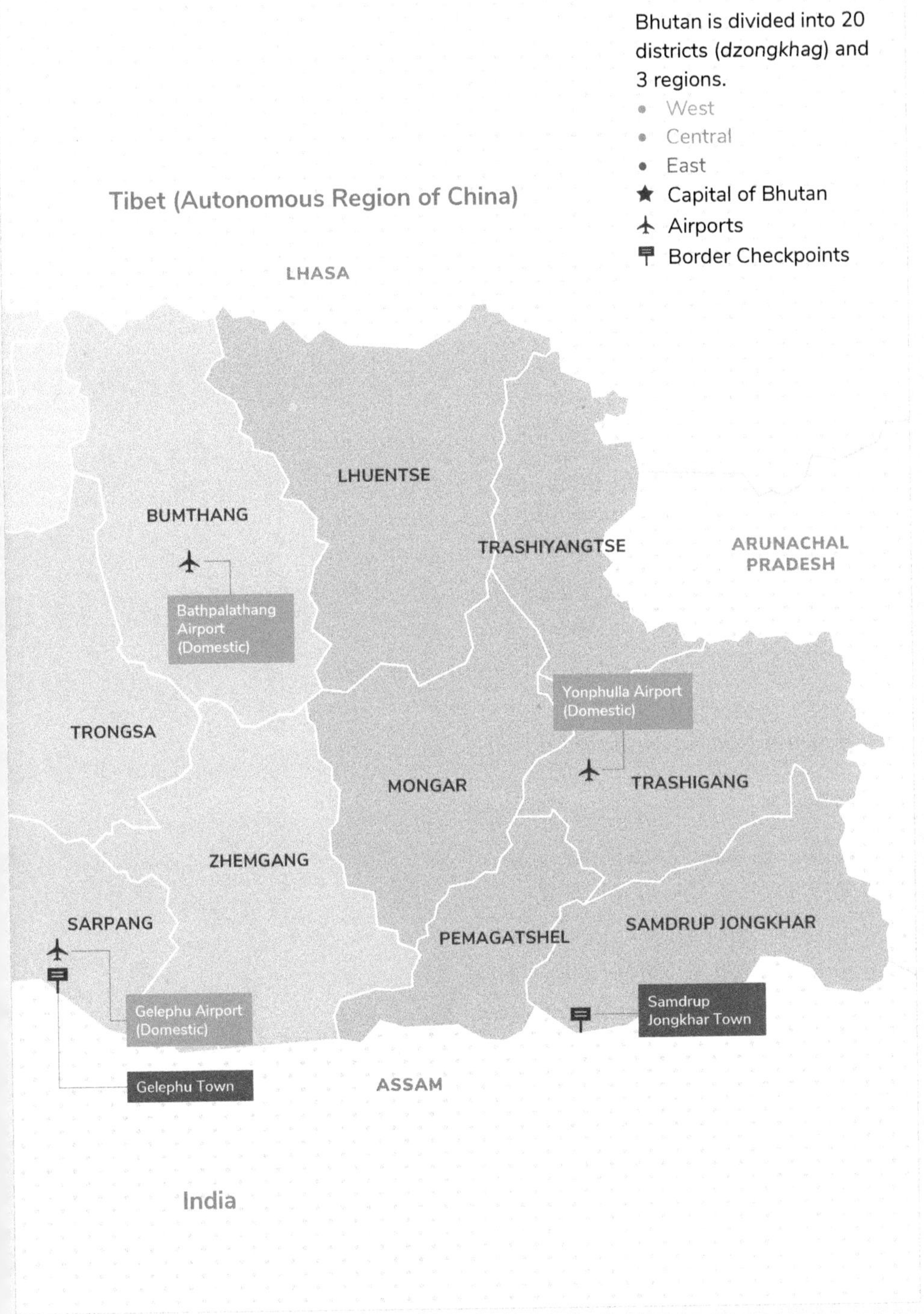

Bhutan is divided into 20 districts (dzongkhag) and 3 regions.

- West
- Central
- East
- ★ Capital of Bhutan
- ✈ Airports
- ⚑ Border Checkpoints

Tibet (Autonomous Region of China)

LHASA

LHUENTSE

BUMTHANG

TRASHIYANGTSE

ARUNACHAL PRADESH

Bathpalathang Airport (Domestic)

Yonphulla Airport (Domestic)

TRONGSA

MONGAR

✈ TRASHIGANG

ZHEMGANG

SARPANG

PEMAGATSHEL

SAMDRUP JONGKHAR

Gelephu Airport (Domestic)

Samdrup Jongkhar Town

Gelephu Town

ASSAM

India

Bhutan is also known as
Druk Yul — Land of Thunder Dragon.

Bhutan, officially known as the **Kingdom of Bhutan**, is a landlocked country in South Asia. The kingdom is sandwiched between two giant countries — China in the north and India in the south. Located in the Eastern Himalayas, Bhutan is bordered by the Tibet Autonomous Region of China in the north, Sikkim (India) and Chumbi Valley (Tibet) in the west, Arunachal Pradesh (India) in the east, as well as Assam (India) and West Bengal (India) in the south.

Bhutan has a total land area of around 38,400 km² with elevations ranging from 300 m in the southern foothills to 7,000 m in the north.

The country is surrounded by the Himalayas in the north and west. The highest point in Bhutan is Gangkhar Puensum, which has the distinction of being the highest unclimbed mountain in the world, at 7,570 m.

The word *druk* or 'thunder dragon' first originated in Tibet. Legend has it that Tsangpa Gyarey, a renowned meditation master and ancestor of Bhutan's founding father, Zhabdrung Ngawang Namgyal, was visiting Nam Village in Lhasa, Tibet to set up a spiritual centre. On his visit there, he was

reported to have seen nine dragons flying, triggering a clap of booming thunder in the sky as he approached them. Reading all these as auspicious omens, he named the centre Druk, and his spiritual tradition took the derivative name Drukpa.

Local historians claim that Bhutan was called Drukyul and her people Drukpa after most people converted to the Drukpa school of Buddhism. Before becoming Druk Yul, Bhutan was known as Lho Jong 'The Valleys of the South' or Lho Jong Menjong 'The Southern Valleys of Medicinal Herbs'.

Bhutan is also known to be one of the world's last surviving Buddhist kingdom. And some say, the last Shangri-La.

The Kingdom of Bhutan made international headlines when it became a democratic, constitutional monarchy in 2008.

Majestic Gangkhar Phuensum with its towering peaks

National Symbols

National Flag

Bhutan's national flag is divided diagonally into two halves of yellow and orange. The upper half in yellow symbolises the king as the upholder of the spiritual and secular foundations of Bhutan. The lower orange symbolises the flourishing of Buddhist teachings, manifested in the Drukpa Kagyu and Nyingmapa traditions. The dragon signifies the name and purity of the country: Druk Yul, Land of Thunder Dragon, while the jewels in its claws denote the country's wealth and perfection.

National Emblem

The national emblem of Bhutan maintains some of the emblems of the national flag. It is contained in a circle with a crossed *dorje* (thunderbolts) in the centre, placed above a lotus and flanked by two thunder dragons. In the compassionate form of Triple Gem, the sacred jewel at the top of the royal crest symbolises the supremacy of the sovereign in the Buddhist Kingdom of Bhutan while the lotus represents purity.

The crossed dorjes placed above the lotus represent the harmonious relationship between the traditional customs of spiritual law and modern authority. The male and female thunder dragons with snarling mouths symbolise the country's guardian deities protecting the country.

Climate

Bhutan has a variety of climates due to varying altitudes and terrain. The south has a hot and humid subtropical climate, and the southern foothills experience the heaviest rainfall due to the southwest monsoon flowing from the Bay of Bengal. The west-central part has temperate climates with warm summers, and cool winters with snowfall occurring occasionally. In the northern region, the weather is much colder during winter. Mountain peaks are perpetually covered in snow, while lower parts are still cool during summer due to the high altitude.

Seasons

Bhutan has four distinct seasons. Spring in Bhutan is relatively short. It usually starts in early March and lasts until mid-April. Summer with occasional showers happens from mid-April until late June, whereas heavier summer rain lasts from late June until late September. Autumn follows until late November, and winter sets in from then until March.

Population

Bhutan has a population of 779,450 people (as of June 2021), which is equivalent to 0.01% of the total world population. The population density in Bhutan is 20 people per km². Nearly half, or 45.8% of the population lives in urban areas.

The Bhutanese

Ngalop, Sharchokpa and Lhotshampa

There are three major ethnic groups in Bhutan: Ngalop, Sharchokpa and Lhotshampa. They are also collectively known as Drukpas (literally, people from Bhutan).

Aside from the three major ethnic groups, Bhutan has nomadic communities living in the highlands such as the Brokpas in the east, and the Layaps and Lunaps in the northern part of Bhutan.

National Language

Dzongkha

The national language of Bhutan is Dzongkha. There are two other major languages, Tshanglakha and Lotshamkha. In total, there are 19 different languages and dialects spoken throughout the country.

Spiritual Practices

Buddhism

Bhutanese predominantly practice Vajrayana Buddhism (Drukpa Kagyu and Nyingmapa traditions).

National Animal

Takin

Bhutan's national animal is the takin (*Budorcas taxicolor*), a rare mammal that is often associated with religious history and mythology. There is a takin preserve in Motithang in Thimphu, where tourists can visit to catch a glimpse of this unique national animal.

National Flower

Himalayan Blue Poppy

The national flower of Bhutan is the Himalayan blue poppy (*Meconopsis gakyidiana*). It is a rare flower that grows at an elevation of 3,700 - 4,300 metres above sea level. The elusive Himalayan blue poppies can be found in eastern Bhutan, particularly in Merak and Sakteng.

National Tree

Himalayan Cypress

The national tree of Bhutan is the Himalayan cypress (*Cupressus torulosa*). Cypresses are found in abundance and easily noticeable near temples and monasteries. The cypresses grow in temperate climate zones between 1,800 - 3,500 metres.

National Bird

Raven

The national bird of Bhutan is the raven. It represents one of the most powerful deities of the country, Jarog Dongchen.

The Royal Raven Crown worn by the kings of Bhutan represents the deep reverence that Bhutanese hold for these national birds as protective deities.

National Sport

Archery

Archery was declared the national sport in 1971 when Bhutan became a member of the United Nations. Bhutan also maintains an Olympics archery team.

Bhutanese regularly hold archery competitions and tournaments throughout the country. The target distance for archery in Bhutan is 145 metre, double that of an Olympics archery range.

National Butterfly

Ludlow's Bhutan Swallowtail

Ludlow's Bhutan swallowtail was originally discovered by botanists Frank Ludlow and George Sheriff in Bhutan around 1933-1934. It was rediscovered 75 years later by Karma Wangdi, a forestry officer, in August 2009. He collected the first evidence — a specimen of the butterfly — in Bumdeling Wildlife Sanctuary and proved that this rare butterfly can still be found in Bhutan. Ludlow's Bhutan swallowtail (*Bhutanitis ludlow*) was officially endorsed as the national butterfly in 2012.

History of Bhutan

Early History

Bhutan's vibrant history is strongly tied to Buddhism. You'll discover important spiritual masters of the Himalayas who played vital roles in Bhutan's early history. When trying to understand Bhutan's history, you have to open up your mind. Instead of rationalising the events, we suggest you visualise the essence of its spirituality. Absorb the interesting folklores about the kingdom.

Buddhism was first introduced to Bhutan in the 7th century when the Tibetan King, Songtsen Gampo, built Kyichu Lhakhang in Paro and Jambay Lhakhang in Bumthang — two of the 108 temples built to pin down a demoness.

It is believed that the demoness was obstructing the spread of Buddhism, and these two temples pinned down the left foot and left knee of the demoness who was subdued.

The Zhabdrung and the Dual System of Government, 1600 - 1907

Under the politically and religiously charismatic Ngawang Namgyal, Bhutan became a unified polity in the 17th century. Ngawang Namgyal was a religious master of the Drukpa school who held the honorary title of Zhabdrung Rinpoche, 'Precious Jewel at Whose Feet One Prostrates'. Persecuted in Tibet, he fled to Bhutan in 1616. Over the next 30 years, he unified the 'southern valleys' into the nation State of Druk Yul.

Zhabdrung Ngawang Namgyal provided Bhutan with a unique system of administration and law. He established the unique system of government with the Central Monastic Body under a religious leader, the Je Khenpo (chief abbot), and a political system administered by a temporal chief, the desi (secular ruler). This dual system of government, choesi, lasted until the Wangchuck dynasty took over in 1907.

You may see children as young as seven years old enrolled in a monastic school

Painting of Zhabdrung Ngawang Namgyal

Bhutan and the British

The 200 years prior to the establishment of the monarchy was the most unstable period in the history of Bhutan, with internal strife, civil wars and political turmoil. 22 desis were reported to be assassinated or deposed by rivals during these years, except for the 13th desi, Sheru Wangchuk, who ruled for 20 years. Between 1651 and 1730, Tibet invaded Bhutan around seven times. The political instability caused rival factions to seek support from the Chinese emperor in Beijing.

In 1730, the 10th desi, Mipham Wangmo, assisted Gya Chila, the ruler of Cooch Behar (present-day West Bengal), against intrusion in a family feud, thus allowing Bhutan to station a force in Cooch Behar. In 1768, the desi formed alliances with the Panchen Lama in Tibet and King Prithvi Narayan Shah of Nepal.

In 1772, Bhutan invaded Cooch Behar to help settle a feud over succession, resulting in Cooch Behar seeking assistance from the British East India Company. British East India Company drove the Bhutanese garrison out of Cooch Behar and later attacked Bhutan itself in 1773. The Druk Desi signed a Treaty of Peace with the British East India Company on April 25, 1774, where Bhutan agreed to return to its pre-1730 boundaries.

The Duar War

However, skirmishes over boundaries and trading rights continued with the British for the next 100 years. The continual skirmishes at the southern border escalated and eventually led to the Duar War (1864-1865), a confrontation over who would control the Bengal Duars. Bengal Duars is the area of plains between the Brahmaputra River up to the lowest hills of Bhutan.

The Duar War lasted only five months. It ended in Bhutan's defeat and loss of the Assam Duars and Bengal Duars. On November 11, 1865, Bhutan signed the Treaty of Sinchula to restore friendly relations and gave up the territories in exchange for an annuity from the British.

During this period, there was a civil war in Bhutan due to power struggles between the Paro and Trongsa valleys. The Trongsa's penlop (governor), Jigme Namgyal, eventually controlled central and eastern Bhutan. After his death, he was succeeded by his son, Ugyen Wangchuck, who defeated his political rivals in several civil wars, and was elected as the first hereditary King of Bhutan, marking the beginning of the Wangchuck dynasty.

Monarchy and Governance

In 2008, Bhutan became a constitutional monarchy, with His Majesty the fifth King as the Head of State. The kings of Bhutan are known as Druk Gyalpo, 'Dragon King'. Through the admirable stewardship of the Druk Gyalpos, Bhutan has shown excellent leadership in environmental preservation and balanced governance. They have maintained significant forest cover, provided a safe habitat for endangered species, and adopted many environmentally friendly and sustainable policies.

Ugyen Wangchuck

FIRST KING (1862 - 1926)

Ugyen Wangchuck was unanimously elected as the hereditary ruler of Bhutan by Bhutan's chiefs and principal lamas on December 17, 1907. He was crowned the Head of State and given the title Druk Gyalpo, ending the *choesi*, dual system of government.

The first King had developed close relations with the British by assisting in negotiations between Britain and Tibet. He was deeply aware that Bhutan would need support through times of regional conflict and rivalries.

During his reign, Bhutan remained largely isolated from the rest of the world.

Ugyen Wangchuck died in 1926 and was succeeded by his son, Jigme Wangchuck.

Jigme Wangchuck

SECOND KING (1905 - 1952)

Jigme Wangchuck became the second King of Bhutan in 1926 after the death of his father.

Jigme Wangchuck's reign saw significant administrative reforms in the country. He enforced a hierarchical system where the king had absolute power over all religious and secular matters. He also appointed a chief abbot to set up a central religious administrative body.

He is often credited for bringing modern education to Bhutan. In 1949, he signed the Indo-Bhutan Treaty with India, calling for peace between the two nations and reinforcing Bhutan's sovereignty and independence. He also continued his father's legacy by maintaining the country's isolation and ensuring political stability.

Jigme Dorji Wangchuck

THIRD KING (1929 - 1972)

Jigme Dorji Wangchuck, also fondly known as the Father of Modern Bhutan, succeeded the throne in 1952 following his father's death. He opened up Bhutan to the outside world, embarked on modernisation and kickstarted Bhutan's journey towards democracy. His education in England and exposure to many foreign countries provided him with broader political and economic perspectives. In 1953, he introduced democratic institutions in Bhutan including the *Tshogdu* (National Assembly), which had the power to remove the king or his successors with a two-thirds majority.

He formulated a new legal and judicial system and drafted the country's first economic development plan. He also developed Bhutan's infrastructure, including the transportation, education, communications, agriculture, and healthcare systems.

Jigme Dorji Wangchuck was the driving force behind the modern education system in Bhutan. More notably, Bhutan's isolation from the world ended under his reign. He viewed diplomatic relationships with other countries as integral to Bhutan's sovereignty and independence.

He died from a heart ailment on July 21, 1972, in Nairobi, Kenya, at the age of 43.

Jigme Singye Wangchuck

FOURTH KING (1955 - PRESENT, abdicated in 2006)

Jigme Singye Wangchuck assumed power in 1972 at the tender age of 17 following the sudden death of his father. Despite his youthfulness and lack of experience, he brought profound wisdom to the throne. He focused on economic self-reliance while preserving the culture, tradition, and natural environment of Bhutan. He also coined the renowned 'Gross National Happiness' philosophy to measure society's progress and development instead of Gross National Product. Bhutan's economy accelerated under his reign, during which he established industries in raw materials, agriculture and hydropower.

The King also focused on preserving and promoting national identity as part of the sixth Five-Year Plan introduced in 1987. He recognised that a solid distinct national identity was crucial for Bhutan's well-being and security. As part of the 'One Nation, One People' policy, the King issued a royal decree to strengthen the Bhutanese identity by promoting the Bhutanese etiquette, national dress and national language.

The far-sighted king also promulgated the 'High value, Low volume' tourism policy in the 1970s. This policy led to the strategy of avoiding mass tourism in Bhutan, to ensure economic returns while preserving the culture and environment.

Jigme Khesar Namgyel Wangchuck

FIFTH KING (1980 - PRESENT)

Jigme Khesar Namgyel Wangchuck ascended the throne on November 6, 2008. He was educated in India and the United States before attending Oxford University, where he studied politics and international relations. After his coronation, he launched the National Cadastral Resurvey, which focuses on improving the lives of Bhutanese living in remote areas.

He signed a new Treaty of Friendship with India in February 2007, replacing a 1949 treaty. He has launched numerous projects to inspire the elected government to address critical issues in governance, education, the rule of law, media, sustainable economic development, and preservation of the country's environmental and cultural heritage.

Jigme Khesar personally oversaw the peaceful transition from an absolute monarchy into a vibrant constitutional monarchy, just like his father had envisioned. The fifth King is popular and well-loved at home and abroad.

Along with Queen Jetsun Pema, the King travels internationally, raising the profile of Bhutan as a sovereign country. His humble and down-to-earth personality has earned him the title of 'People's King'.

In 2011, the King launched *Desuung* 'Guardians of Peace', a voluntary programme to encourage citizens to play an active role in nation-building by equipping them with skills and knowledge of disaster management. It's one of the most successful initiatives in the kingdom, and more than 22,000 volunteers have been trained under the programme.

During the 112th National Day address in 2019, the King announced that in 2022, Bhutan would kickstart *Gyalsung* (national service) for all Bhutanese who have reached the age of 18. Unlike national service in other countries that are mainly military-focused, the national service in Bhutan focuses on developing the skills and knowledge of the youths.

In 2020, during the coronavirus outbreak that affected the world, the King was at the forefront of the COVID-19 pandemic response in Bhutan. He provided extraordinary leadership and support to keep the people safe from the COVID-19 virus. Taking personal risks, he often toured the country to inspect preparations at vital locations. Upon his command, the Druk Gyalpo's Relief Kidu was set up to grant financial support to assist Bhutanese affected by the pandemic.

> **"** Throughout my reign, I will never rule you as a king. I will protect you as a parent, care for you as a brother and serve you as a son. I shall give you everything and keep nothing; I shall live such a life as a good human being that you may find it worthy to serve as an example for your children; I have no personal goals other than to fulfill your hopes and aspirations. I shall always serve, day and night, in the spirit of kindness, justice and equality. **"**

Royal Family of Bhutan

King Jigme Khesar Namgyel Wangchuck married a commoner, Jetsun Pema, whom he first met at a family gathering when he was 17 years old. Then 7-year-old Jetsun was captivated by the crown prince without knowing his identity.

Like a fairytale, both of them reunited many years later, fell in love and got married after dating for some time.

The royal couple has two adorable sons. Prince Jigme Namgyel Wangchuck, born in 2016, is the official heir to the throne. Prince Jigme Ugyen Wangchuck, born in March 2020, is the latest addition to the royal family.

The royal family is a beacon of hope and a unifying force in the kingdom.

Queen Jetsun Pema

On 13 October, 2011, Jetsun Pema was officially crowned the Queen of Bhutan at the age of 21 upon marrying King Jigme Khesar Namgyel Wangchuck. The world's youngest queen has often been praised for her beauty, kindness, intelligence and elegance. The beautiful Queen is an inspiration to all the women in Bhutan.

Find out more about Queen Jetsun Pema

s.bn.sg/jetsunpema

You can find portraits of the King and the royal family inside all the Bhutanese homes

Constitutional Monarchy

The modern political history of Bhutan is unique. Unlike many other countries where democracy was pursued by popular movements or civil wars, democracy in Bhutan was bestowed from the throne; Jigme Singye Wangchuck initiated the transition from absolute monarchy to constitutional monarchy through a royal decree.

On January 16, 2006, the Election Commission of Bhutan (ECB) was established to organise national elections including basic electoral education, promoting political awareness, and creating an effective voter registration system. It also held two mock elections to give the people a chance to familiarise themselves with the electoral mechanisms and the electronic voting machines. The democratisation process transformed the Bhutanese political system.

The first National Assembly elections in Bhutan took place on March 24, 2008. Two political parties contested in the landmark elections.

The Parliament of Bhutan has two houses: the National Council, which is a house of review, and the National Assembly. The National Council has 25 non-partisan members whereby the people elect 20 members, one for each of the 20 dzongkhags (districts), and the king appoints 5 eminent members. The members serve five-year terms.

The National Assembly has 47 members elected directly by the citizens through their constituencies. The leader of the party that wins majority seats in the National Assembly becomes the prime minister, also known as *lyonchhen*. The prime minister is supported by 10 cabinet ministers. All ministers must be natural-born citizens of Bhutan, and there is a limit of two ministers from any one *dzongkhag*.

On July 18, 2008, the fifth King, Jigme Khesar Namgyel Wangchuck, signed the Constitution, formally marking the end of a century of absolute monarchy in Bhutan.

Proverb

ཡེ་ཤེས་པའི་མདའ་ན་རྒྱབ་སར་མི་མཐོང་ཕོག་སར་མཐོང་།

Ye shey pi da chap sar mi thoeng; phog sar thoeng.

The arrow of the accomplished master will not be seen when it is released; only when it hits the target.

People and National Identity

Bhutan is remarkable in many ways. The Royal Government of Bhutan has prioritised sustaining both tangible and intangible aspects of its culture and national identity. Many unique elements bound the people together, from national dress to their world-class architectural design.

Just greet the Bhutanese with 'kuzuzangpo la' and you'll receive a warm smile in return

Demography of Bhutan

As of 2021, Bhutan has a population of around 780,000 people. The population density in Bhutan is 20 people per km² (52 people per mi²). 45.8% of the population live in urban areas (around 353,445 people) and the median age in Bhutan is 28.1 years old.

The country's inhabitants can be divided into three major ethnic groups: Ngalops in the west, Sharchops in the east and Lhotshampas in the south. However, Bhutanese are also collectively known as Drukpas, 'people from Bhutan'.

The Ngalops are Buddhists who originated from Tibet and primarily settled in the mountainous western region. In the 1850s, a group of Hindu foresters from Nepal migrated to Bhutan and began settling in the lowland regions of southern Bhutan. Thereafter, Indian and Nepalese workers were recruited to help implement the first Five-Year Plan in 1961. They are referred to as Lhotshampas, literally 'people from the southern border'. Meanwhile, the Sharchops are of mixed Tibetan, South Asian, and Southeast Asian descent that mostly live in the eastern districts of Bhutan.

In 1987, the fourth King, Jigme Singye Wangchuck, introduced the 'One Nation, One People' policy under the sixth Five-Year Plan to preserve and maintain the national identity of Bhutan. Subsequently, in 1989, as a part of this policy, he issued a kasho (royal decree) to promote driglam namzha (official code of etiquette and dress code), as well as the Dzongkha language to strengthen Bhutan's unique national identity.

Bhutanese are proud of their culture and traditions. It is visible in how they dress, their architecture, and their interdependence with the natural environment. Therefore, it is not surprising that cultural preservation is one of the main pillars of Bhutan's Gross National Happiness (GNH) philosophy.

Proverb

བསམ་པ་བཟང་ན་ས་དང་ལམ་ཡང་བཟང་། བསམ་པ་ངན་ན་ས་དང་ལམ་ཡང་ངན།

Sampa zang na sa dang lam yang zang; sampa nyen na sa dang lam yang nyen.

If the thought is good, your place and path are good;
if the thought is bad, your place and path are bad.

Driglam Namzha

Driglam namzha, in essence, is the conduct of oneself. It focuses on certain physical, verbal and mental etiquette. It also emphasises good manners when alone or in the company of others. The practice of driglam namzha is a characteristic of the Bhutanese culture and identity. Every Bhutanese is taught the norms and practices from a young age and everyone is expected to have a basic understanding of it.

The history of this cultural etiquette dates back to the 17th century when Zhabdrung Ngawang Namgyal promoted the practices to establish order and unify the country. After the royal decree issued by the fourth King in 1989, driglam namzha became an official protocol, with a set of ceremonial conduct that is strictly adhered to by all citizens.

Ultimately, driglam namzha promotes values such as humility, self-control, and compassion while also displaying sensitivity and respect towards others. Some examples of behaviour include walking behind high officials, not sitting cross-legged in front of superiors, and bowing in the presence of the king or other high officials.

Driglam means 'order, discipline, custom, rules, regimen'. **Namzha** means 'system'. Driglam Namzha governs how citizens dress in public and behave in official settings.

Bhutanese women looking beautiful in their bright kiras and rachus

National Dress

Bhutan's national dress is deemed very important for the preservation of its culture and national identity. Bhutanese take great pride in wearing their traditional clothing, and you can see them wearing the dress in daily life.

The traditional dress for men is the gho, a knee-length robe tied with a handwoven belt, known as kera. Under the gho, men wear a tegu, a white jacket with long, folded-back cuffs.

Women wear the kira, a large rectangular cloth held together by a koma (brooch). The kira is often worn with colourful blouses called wonju alongside a tego (an outer jacket).

The textiles are mostly handwoven and intricately designed by talented weavers throughout the country.

You can see the locals in their finest attires during special occasions such as weddings and festivals.

When visiting a dzong or government office flying the national flag, the Bhutanese wear the national dress with ceremonial scarves. Men will wear a kabney (silk scarf) from left shoulder to the hip, and women drape a rachu, a narrow embroidered cloth, over their left shoulder.

Bhutanese men looking suave in their ghos and white kabneys

Ceremonial Scarves in Bhutan

The rank of the person determines the colour of the kabney and rachu that a Bhutanese wears.

Photos are for illustration purposes only. These are the more common scarfs that you'll see in Bhutan but there are other coloured scarfs that represent the different ranks.

- Saffron - **His Majesty the King and the Chief Abbot** (*Je Khenpo*).
- Orange - **Ministers.**
- Red (*bura marp*) or Red-gold (*lungmar*) - *Dasho*, **an honorary title conferred by the king.**
- Green - **Judges.**
- Blue - **Members of the National Assembly and National Council.**

- White with fringes and a red band with one, two or three red stripes - **District administrators and governors** (Dzongrab, Dungpa).
- White with fringes and two broad, red, vertical borders (*khamar*) - **Village chiefs** (Gups).
- White **for males and** colourful **for females** - Commoner.

Bhutanese in their beautiful traditional dress are a common sight in Bhutan

 Tips

Foreigners and tourists are not required to adhere to the strict dress code when entering the dzong, temples or monasteries but are required to dress decently such as tops with sleeves and long pants. However, you will need to remove your shoes and headgear.

Check out how to wear a full kira

s.bn.sg/kira

Livelihood

Bhutan remains a largely rural and agrarian economy. As in many developing countries, agro-pastoralism is the major form of livelihood for rural communities. As such, agriculture is the main livelihood for more than half of the Bhutanese population. The majority of the Bhutanese live in small rural villages along the mountainous ridges and river valleys. Traditionally they were a subsistence farming population, largely self-sufficient in food: growing their own crops and grazing animals for meat, butter, cheese and milk. Work is often communal, and there is usually a cooperative environment in the village to help farmers sow and harvest their crops.

The other primary sources of income for Bhutanese are tourism, hydropower and public sectors, including civil service, government agencies and the armed forces.

A Bhutanese woman removing chaff from rice using the traditional method

Houses and Architecture

Houses in Bhutan are traditionally built with stone, wood and rammed earth that may rise as high as three storeys. Lively and colourful motifs adorn the homes.

The traditional houses are an architectural feat as they are constructed entirely without nails, just like their magnificent fortresses. Heavy stones hold the shingled roofs to prevent them from being swept away by strong winds. Windows are made up of sliding panels, and narrow stairs connect one floor to the next. The ground floor houses domestic animals and a storage area, while the first floor is the living quarters and kitchen.

The top floor is the most important part of the house. There is usually a choesum, an elaborately decorated shrine room with an altar.

With modernisation, building materials became readily available. The new houses are made up of cement, bricks, stones and sand, and the roofs of corrugated galvanised iron sheets.

You can also find thatched bamboo houses in the lower altitudes in the southern region of Bhutan. Meanwhile, the semi-nomadic yak herders in the northern region live in tiny stone houses or yak-hair tents as they move across the pasture land.

Designs of traditional buildings in Bhutan must adhere to strict cultural guidelines

A traditional Bhutanese house with idyllic surroundings in Chumey, Bumthang

Food and Drink

Bhutanese cuisine is influenced by Chinese, Tibetan and Indian cuisines. However, as Bhutanese food habits and dishes continue to evolve, Bhutan develops its own distinctive flavours.

Contrary to popular belief, not all Bhutanese are vegetarians. A large part of the population still enjoys eating meat even though Bhutan is a predominantly Buddhist country.

Beef and **pork** as air dried meats are commonly served in Bhutan, and **yak meat** from the highlanders is a delicacy. Fish are rare in Bhutan as there are strict regulations on fishing in the country but farmed freshwater trout is becoming popular.

Some popular meat dishes include **shakam paa** (dried beef), **sikkam paa** (desiccated thin sliced pork) and **jasha maru** (chicken stew).

A common ingredient that runs through most Bhutanese food is **chilli peppers.** While you are in Bhutan, expect to see bright red peppers drying on roofs under the sun.

Bhutanese eat many plant-based foods such as wild mushrooms, sweet potatoes, tender bamboo shoots, fiddlehead ferns, nettle flowers, and orchid flower buds.

Some authentic Bhutanese dishes that you can find in a staple diet include a mountain of rice, usually healthy red rice, **ema datshi** (chilli cheese), and **ezay** (chilli condiment).

Ema datshi is a traditional Bhutanese stew made up of ema (chillies) and datshi (yak cheese). It is deemed the national dish of Bhutan, and is loved by both locals and tourists alike. **Kewa datshi (**potato cheese)

and **shamu datshi** (mushroom cheese) are other delicious Bhutanese dishes.

A popular breakfast choice in Bhutan is **khur-le** (buckwheat pancake). Meanwhile, during winter, **bathuk** (wheat flour noodle soup) is a favourite for Bhutanese to keep themselves warm.

Just like the Nepalis, Bhutanese also enjoy eating steamed dumplings, locally known as **momos.** You can easily find meat or vegetable dumplings all over the country.

You can also find garlands of **chugo** (hardened cheese) hanging outside grocery stores. Chugo is made from yak's milk, air-dried until it becomes hard like a rock. Don't worry if you have difficulty sucking chugo; it is known to be the hardest cheese in the world!

Some Bhutanese also love chewing **doma** (areca nut) wrapped in betel leaves with a dash of slaked lime after a meal. Doma is addictive for its stimulant effects. It is an acquired taste, somewhat bitter, and chewing too much of it can turn your teeth and lips red. The locals may offer you doma as a customary greeting, or polite social gesture.

Suja (butter tea) is often served on all social occasions along with some **zaw** (roasted rice). **Ara** — a spirit distilled from rice, maize, wheat or barley — is also one of the Bhutanese's favourite beverages.

There are also locally produced alcoholic beverages such as Red Panda, Druk 11000, Bhutanese Red-Rice Lager and more. Many alcohol lovers sing praises for the Zumzin peach wine and K5 whiskeys.

Bhutan is a paradise for spicy food lovers

Doma is the culprit for all the red-stained teeth

Chicken stew is a popular Bhutanese dish

Tea time usually means butter tea and roasted rice

Try biting into the hardest cheese in the world

Savour the taste of dried pork with chillies

Traditional Eating Habits in Bhutan

Mealtimes are social affairs in Bhutan. When eating in a group, Bhutanese traditionally observe the *driglam namzha* and are expected to sit cross-legged in a circle on the floor. In the past, the head of the family is served first, and no one can leave until all the family members finish eating. Silence is to be maintained while eating. However, these traditional practices are fading over time. These days, mealtimes are no longer quiet, and laughter is shared instead.

Traditionally, dishes were served in *dapas* (wooden bowls), but with the easy availability of modern goods, modern ceramic bowls have replaced the wooden bowls. Similarly, *bangchungs* — circular containers made from special bamboo called *yura* — were also used to serve rice and other dry snacks. Bhutanese rarely use these traditional products now, but you can still find conventional *dapas* or *bangchungs* sold in many handicraft shops.

Back in the day, Bhutanese used to eat with their hands while sitting on the floor. With modernisation, eating habits have changed and evolved. In urban areas, Bhutanese usually eat with cutleries and on regular dining tables. Nowadays, you will usually find Bhutanese eating with their hands only when they are at home or having a picnic.

Stir-fried noodles is an Asian delicacy

The locals enjoy eating pork dishes

Potato cheese in Bhutan is a must-try

Chilli cheese is a celebrated dish in Bhutan

Buckwheat dumplings are a unique local specialty

Religions, Customs and Traditions

> " While Buddhism is widely practiced in Bhutan, about 20% of the population practice Hinduism, especially amongst the Lhotshampas. Christians are present in small numbers. "

Buddhism in Bhutan

Bhutan is the only country in the world where Vajrayana Buddhism, known as the 'Thunderbolt Vehicle' or 'Diamond Vehicle', is practiced as the state religion. Ever since Buddhism was introduced to the country, religion has been very prevalent in every facet of Bhutanese life. Buddhist values are often inculcated in the younger generations during their formative years.

Buddhism originated from the teachings of Siddharta Gautama, also known as Shakyamuni Buddha, a royal prince from the Shakya clan in the 6th century BCE. When Gautama stumbled upon human sufferings outside of his palace, he renounced all worldly pleasures and embarked on a spiritual quest to seek solutions to the suffering. After years of rigorous contemplation and meditation, he gained enlightenment while meditating under a ficus tree, known as 'The Bodhi Tree'.

Following the Buddha's passing, different schools of thought appeared amongst his disciples, influencing their interpretation of the doctrines. There are two principal schools of Buddhism, Mahayana and Hinayana — sometimes referred to as Theravada.

In addition, Vajrayana (tantrism) emerged as a branch of Mahayana teachings. Over the centuries, Vajrayana in Tibet gradually divided into four major schools: Nyingmapa, Kagyupa, Sakyapa and Gelugpa. Nyingmapa is the oldest sect that traces its origin back to the teachings of the great Indian saint Guru Padmasambhava, popularly known as Guru Rinpoche.

Buddhist teachings of compassion are the basis for Bhutanese religious beliefs and practices. The majority of the Bhutanese population follow either the Drukpa Kagyu or Nyingma sect. The people in central and eastern Bhutan widely follow Nyingmapa, whereas the people from the western region practice Drukpa Kagyu.

Prayer wheels are inscribed with sacred mantras

Spinning the prayer wheels can bring enlightenment to all sentient beings

It's common for monks to join the monastery at a very young age

The offering of butter lamps is a usual spiritual practice for Bhutanese

The sight of fluttering colourful prayer flags in Bhutan has a calming effect

Monks play the *dungchen* — a long horn or trumpet — during ceremonies

Guru Rinpoche

An Indian Tantric Master Padmasambhava, popularly known as 'Guru Rinpoche', is one of Bhutan's most important historical and religious figures. His first visit to Bumthang in 746 AD is considered a turning point in the country's history and the actual introduction of Vajrayana Buddhism to Bhutan. The King of Bumthang invited Guru Rinpoche to visit his land to subdue and tame demons, subsequently converting them to deities who protect the different valleys in Bhutan. You can find statues of Guru Rinpoche in almost all the Bhutanese temples throughout the country built after his first visit.

He is said to have eight manifestations and personifies the guru principle — known as the 'Second Buddha' — as prophesied by Sakyamuni, the historical Buddha. He is also regarded as the founder of the Nyingma school, the oldest religious sect of Vajrayana Buddhism. Guru Rinpoche preserved his teachings and wisdom by concealing terma (hidden treasures) in caves, rocks, and lakes to be discovered by future tertons (treasure revealers). One of the most important tertons in Bhutan is Pema Lingpa, who found many statues, scrolls and sacred relics during his time.

Guru Rinpoche visited Bhutan a second time via Singye Dzong in Lhuentse in eastern Bhutan. He left a body print and an impression of his head with a hat at Gom Kora in Trashiyangtse, eastern Bhutan. He flew in the form of Dorje Drolö, one of his eight manifestations, on the back of a flaming tigress to Taktsang in Paro, giving the famous monastery the name 'Tiger's Nest'. The monastery is one of Guru Rinpoche's most sacred sites as he concealed many profound treasures at Taktsang.

A huge statue of Guru Rinpoche in Lhuentse

Guru Rinpoche was often represented in his manifestation as Padmasambhava, wearing the dark blue gown of a mantra practitioner, the red and yellow shawl of a monk, the maroon cloak of a king, and the red robe and white undergarments of a bodhisattva.

Snow-covered Taktsang Monastery during winter season

The Drukpa Kagyu

The eminent religious master Tsangpa Gyare Yeshe Dorje, one of the foremost disciples of Lingje Repa Pema Dorje, founded the Drukpa Kagyu school at the Ralung monastery in Tibet during the 12th century.

Phajo Drugom Zhigpo fulfilled Tsangpa Gyare's prophecy that a young man from eastern Tibet would travel south to spread the Drukpa Kagyu teachings in western Bhutan.

After that, many Buddhist scholars visited Bhutan, but Zhabdrung Ngawang Namgyal's arrival in 1616 established Drukpa Kagyu as the state religion.

Young monks mingling outside the temple

Feel free to interact with the young monks

Women sometimes pray while spinning the wheel

Lama Drukpa Kuenley

Of the numerous saints and scholars who visited Bhutan over the centuries, the Tibetan lama Drukpa Kuenley, from the Drukpa Kagyu lineage, is a popular Buddhist yogi in Bhutanese history.

People remember him for his unorthodox and unconventional teaching methods — usually with bizarre sexual connotations. His 'crazy wisdom' earned him the name 'Divine Madman'.

He was known for using his phallus to awaken unenlightened beings and to subdue demons. Drukpa Kuenley's phallus was so powerful that it is known as the 'Thunderbolt of Flaming Wisdom'. Devotees flock to Chimi Lhakhang, a monastery established to honour Drukpa Kuenley, to offer prayers — many praying specifically for children.

The phallus is now the symbolic reference of fertility and good luck and is a common sight on walls of houses, particularly in western Bhutan. The embellished images are also said to ward off evil spirits.

Painting of a phallus on the wall of a handicraft shop

People from all over the world visit Chimi Lhakhang in Punakha to receive fertility blessings. Many modern miracle babies, sometimes named Chimi or Kinley, have been conceived after their parents received the fertility blessings.

Drukpa Kuenley engraving outside Chimi Lhakhang

The Nyingmapa

The Nyingmapa lineage is the oldest of the major schools of Tibetan Buddhism. It traces its origin to Padmasambhava, who travelled to Tibet at Tibetan King Trisong Deutsen's invitation to help the King establish Buddhism there.

Padmasambhava travelled to Tibet with Shantarakshita, a renowned Buddhist scholar. In Tibet, he pacified the demons, turned them into Dharma protectors and successfully established Buddhism. Padmasambhava had 25 disciples to whom he transmitted the Vajrayana teachings. A vast and complex system of transmission lineages developed from his disciples.

In the early years, the Nyingmapa lineage did not have any proper structure. It relied on oral transmission from master to disciple. The lineage gradually became more institutionalised, and by the 15th century, Tibet had established many monasteries. An important aspect of the Nyingmapa lineage is the transmission of teachings through terma (hidden treasures).

Padmasambhava brought Buddhism to Bhutan in the 8th century and established numerous sacred sites that are important pilgrimage sites today.

There are many types of prayer wheels in Bhutan

Hidden treasures were discovered in the famous Burning Lake of Bumthang

Proverb

ཁ་བདེ་ཁ་གུ་ཆེ་བདེ་ཁ་མ་སྐྱལ།

Kha deu gu chey deu ma kay.

Don't put an easy tongue upon an easy mouth.

Hinduism in Bhutan

While Bhutanese are predominantly Buddhists, the Lhotshampa community in the south are of Nepali and Indian descent who practice Hinduism. Hindus in Bhutan are estimated to be around 20% of the population. Hinduism is one of the world's oldest religions, and its earliest teachings are found in scriptures known as Vedas. The Vedas are amongst the oldest sacred religious texts.

Hinduism has very diverse views on the concept of God. There are six major schools of orthodox Indian Hindu philosophy — Nyaya, Vaisheshika, Samkhya, Yoga, Mīmāṃsā and Vedanta. The major schools of Hindu philosophy explain morality and the nature of existence through the doctrines of samsara, the continuous cycle of life, death and reincarnation, and karma, the universal law of cause and effect. Major Hindu festivals are national holidays in Bhutan.

Devi Panchayan Mandir in Thimphu

Tips

When visiting religious buildings

You should observe a few important rules when visiting a lhakhang (temple) or goemba (monastery).

- You are required to remove your footwear and headgear at the doorway.

- Photography is prohibited inside the temple.

- Ensure that you are dressed appropriately — avoid shorts or sleeveless tops.

- Always move in a clockwise direction when circumambulating a stupa (sacred shrine), chorten (religious structure) or prayer wheel.

- It is customary to leave a small monetary offering on the altar. You should touch the note to your forehead and then place it on the altar. A monk may pour some holy water from a sacred vessel called bumpa, into your hand. You can take a sip of the water and then spread the rest on your head, sweeping from front to back.

- Do not point at any deity, statues, religious artefacts or paintings as it is considered disrespectful. Instead, use an open-palm gesture with your palm up.

- While male visitors may be permitted to enter the goenkhang (inner sanctum), always ask your tour guide before entering. Women are not allowed to enter a goenkhang.

Economy
of Bhutan

Bhutan has one of the world's
smallest economies. They have
sustained growth due to the
development of the hydroelectric
sector and the dynamism of
the tourism sector. Bhutan is
also the first country to use the
Gross National Happiness (GNH)
index to measure the country's
development and progress.

Bhutan's Economy

Significant sectors of Bhutan's economy today consist of forestry, tourism, and hydroelectric power sales. Bhutan also exports cement, dolomite, ferroalloys, agricultural products, handicrafts, and cordyceps sinensis. The rural economy is still primarily based on subsistence agriculture.

Bhutan has one of the world's smallest economies, with the 2020 Gross Domestic Product at around USD2.59bn. Bhutan has an average GDP growth of 7.5%. The hydroelectricity and construction sectors generally contribute over one-third of the GDP, while the rest come from the service and primary sectors.

Bhutan has invested heavily in hydroelectricity to become self-sufficient, intending to generate about 10,000 megawatts of hydropower.

The government actively encourages the development of other sectors, such as waste management, education services, healthcare services and information technology.

There has also been a deliberate focus on attracting foreign investments into several sectors through foreign direct investment (FDI).

> Tourism is another important sector of the economy that generates significant employment for the locals.

A tourist browsing through a handicraft shop

A tourist learning about Bhutan's traditional crafts

A key challenge is the rising youth unemployment. The government has implemented various schemes to support young people: expanding their skill set, identifying avenues for employment, promoting entrepreneurship education, and encouraging self-employment.

Currency

The financial services sector is also evolving. There are four central banks and multiple insurance companies.

The Bank of Bhutan, with headquarters in Phuentsholing, was established by a Royal Charter in 1968, a significant step towards the transition from barter to an entirely monetary system. Today, the Bank of Bhutan has many branches throughout the country.

In 1974, Bhutan introduced the Ngultrum (BTN) as the official currency. The Ngultrum is on par with the Indian Rupee and available in the following denominations: Nu. 1, Nu. 5, Nu. 10, Nu. 20, Nu. 50, Nu. 100, Nu. 500, Nu. 1,000.

 Tips

You are encouraged to bring larger denominations for exchange as larger bills will give you a higher exchange rate. Check out the FAQs (pg. 237) for the currencies that you can exchange in Bhutan. Do note that US Dollar bills issued before the year 2000 are not accepted. Indian Rupees (INR50, INR100 and INR500) are commonly accepted in Bhutan.

Tourism

Tourism in Bhutan is still relatively young: the kingdom first opened to foreign tourists in 1974. In that year, Bhutan received a total of a mere 287 foreign visitors.

However, the tourism industry in the kingdom is vibrant with a high potential for growth. Bhutan's tourism is founded on the principle of sustainability — tourism must be environmentally and ecologically friendly, socially and culturally acceptable, and economically viable. Thus, sustainability is at the core of the 'High value, Low volume' tourism policy implementation. This differentiation from other destinations serves as a competitive advantage for Bhutan as a high-end travel destination.

As part of the policy, the government implements a **Sustainable Development Fee (SDF)**, a tourism levy on all leisure tourists. All tourists other than nationals from India, Bangladesh and Maldives are required to pay a Sustainable Development Fee (SDF) of USD200 per person per night after the Tourism Levy Bill 2022 was passed on 28 June 2022. The tourism levy does not include accommodation, transportation, meals and monument entrance fees that were implemented from September 2022. Aside from that, engaging a tour operator to enter Bhutan is now optional.

For decades, regional tourists from India, Bangladesh and Maldives could enter Bhutan without paying the minimum daily package. However, from July 2020, regional tourists have been required to pay the SDF of Nu. 1200 (approx. USD16) per person per night.

Prior to the border closures due to the COVID-19 pandemic, Bhutan received the highest number of tourists in 2019 with a total of 315,599 visitors. The top 10 tourist arrivals were from the United States of America, China, the United Kingdom, Germany, Australia, Vietnam, Japan, Thailand, Singapore and Malaysia.

Why do you pay the Sustainable Development Fee (SDF)?

1. To contribute to the overall sustainability of tourism in Bhutan.

2. To contribute to the enhancement of infrastructure and facilities, particularly the tourism infrastructure and facilities.

3. To process route permits in advance so that tourists do not have to wait at the border gates when visiting the different districts.

4. To ensure the safety of all tourists through dedicated tour guides.

5. To get preferential exemptions from paying entry fees for state-owned tourist attractions.

6. To receive guaranteed quality services from the hospitality and tourism sector.

The picturesque Phobjikha Valley is well-loved by many tourists

Eastern Bhutan is a paradise for offbeat travellers

Education

Until the 1950s, the form of education available in Bhutan was mainly monastic. The growing influence of the British in the late 19th century influenced Ugyen Wangchuck towards Western-style education. He set up private schools in Haa and Bumthang. Today, there are three primary forms of education in Bhutan: general education, monastic education and non-formal education. General education is currently seen as the formal education structure.

The government encourages Bhutanese to pursue education and provides **free education** to every child of school age. In addition, the government also provides university scholarships to students who excel in their studies.

From 1961 to 2020, the modern education system has expanded from about 11 schools to 1132 schools, including early childhood education, primary schools, secondary schools, technical and vocational institutions, as well as tertiary institutions.

Increasingly, many efforts are focused on providing technical and vocational training to the youths. The government believes that equipping students with relevant skills will help ensure employability in the future.

Bhutan's youth literacy rate (15 - 24 years old) is at 84%, and English has been the medium of instruction since the beginning of modern education.

As a result, most Bhutanese are fluent in English, especially the younger generation.

Bhutanese students enjoy free education in the country

Technology

Unlike most countries that gradually experience technological progression, technology advancement happened rapidly in Bhutan. The kingdom was one of the last countries in the world to introduce television and the Internet in 1999. Given the global trends, the decision to establish technological infrastructure and services was inevitable. Currently, more than 87% of the population has a cell phone.

Recognising the importance of technology, the fifth King constantly emphasises the need to promote technology literacy and skills in Bhutan.

The government inaugurated the first IT park in Thimphu in May 2012. Thimphu Tech Park is the first of its kind in the kingdom. There is also an incubation centre within the park where entrepreneurs can run pilot tests to harness any technology opportunity for Bhutan.

Healthcare

As with education, Bhutan provides **free health care** services to its citizens. Bhutan established modern health care in the early 1960s and since then has made remarkable progress, with more than 90% of the population benefiting from primary health care services. Basic health units (BHU) and outreach clinics bring health care to remote areas. Patients in need of sophisticated and expensive treatments are referred abroad at the government's expense.

The current life expectancy in Bhutan is 72.17 years. In 2020, the infant mortality rate for Bhutan was 22.27 deaths per 1,000 live births, a 3.88% decline from 2019. Bhutan has made major progress in lowering the infant mortality rate. Child immunisation is above 90%, and access to potable water and public sanitation has improved over the years. The government invests a major proportion of its expenditure in education and healthcare.

Bhutan organised the first Startup Weekend in 2016

Primary health care services are free in Bhutan

Gross National Happiness

Most people have probably heard of Bhutan because of its development vision of Gross National Happiness (GNH). This concept was announced by the fourth King, Jigme Singye Wangchuck, in 1979. He believes that happiness should be the goal for human progress instead of GDP.

GNH strives to measure development more holistically, focusing on balancing the people's physical, spiritual, emotional and psychological well-being.

In establishing the GNH Index, Bhutan created a metric to measure the quality of life in terms of happiness.

GNH is perceived as four pillars: good governance, sustainable socio-economic development, cultural preservation and environmental conservation. These are expanded into nine domains, 38 sub-indexes, 72 indicators (33 grouped indicators), and 151 variables to define and analyse the happiness of the Bhutanese.

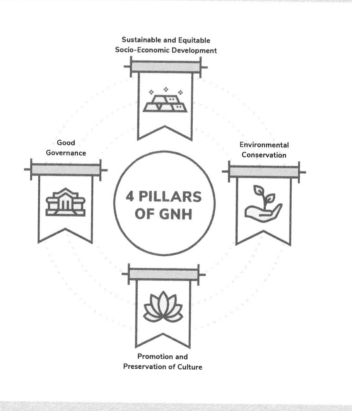

Bhutan carefully plans and executes surveys on five-year cycles in line with its tradition of presenting five-year plans. In the past, the survey could take up to nine hours to complete. They have now condensed it to three hours.

In Bhutan, all government policies and development plans have to align with the fundamental tenets of GNH.

The Gross National Happiness Commission (GNHC) is the government agency tasked with incorporating GNH into policy-making and planning.

In line with the GNH pillars, Bhutan is a world leader in environmental preservation. The kingdom currently holds the title of being the **world's only carbon-negative country.** It absorbs more greenhouse gases in the atmosphere than it emits.

The constitution of Bhutan also mandates that the country maintain a minimum forest cover of 60%. Currently, over 70% of the land is covered by forests, making Bhutan one of the greenest countries in the world.

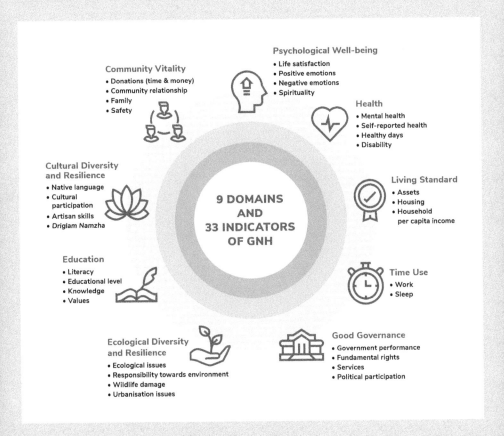

Community Vitality
- Donations (time & money)
- Community relationship
- Family
- Safety

Psychological Well-being
- Life satisfaction
- Positive emotions
- Negative emotions
- Spirituality

Health
- Mental health
- Self-reported health
- Healthy days
- Disability

Cultural Diversity and Resilience
- Native language
- Cultural participation
- Artisan skills
- Driglam Namzha

9 DOMAINS AND 33 INDICATORS OF GNH

Living Standard
- Assets
- Housing
- Household per capita income

Education
- Literacy
- Educational level
- Knowledge
- Values

Time Use
- Work
- Sleep

Ecological Diversity and Resilience
- Ecological issues
- Responsibility towards environment
- Wildlife damage
- Urbanisation issues

Good Governance
- Government performance
- Fundamental rights
- Services
- Political participation

Festivals
of Bhutan

Festivals are one of the most
important aspects of Bhutanese
culture. The kingdom is famous
for its exuberant religious festivals.
These special celebrations carry
a lot of spiritual significance for
the locals.

A dancer wearing a mask of a mythical creature

Tshechus

Every year, thousands of visitors flock to Bhutan's various dzongs to experience the tshechus

Tshechu literally means 'tenth day' and is considered the most important religious festival in Bhutan. It is held annually in the monasteries and dzongs of all the 20 districts. In the different months of the year, the festival honours Guru Rinpoche, who brought Buddhism to Bhutan in the 8th century. A tshechu typically lasts for four or five days. It is celebrated on the tenth day of the Bhutanese lunar calendar, corresponding to the birthday of Guru Rinpoche. Hence, the exact dates of the tshechu in the different districts vary from year to year.

For Bhutanese, attending this religious festival is an integral part of their spiritual devotion to Buddhism. They believe that by attending the festival, they can accumulate spiritual merits and move towards enlightenment, the ultimate goal of Buddhism. Today, tshechus are also important social events in every district.

The popular tshechus for tourists to attend are Paro Tshechu during spring and Thimphu Tshechu and Bumthang Tshechu during autumn.

Cham (Dance)

The highlight of the festival is the sacred *Cham* performances by both laity and monks dressed in ornate costumes. The ancient dances have been transmitted in Bhutan from person-to-person, for hundreds of years. Young monks undergo an extensive apprenticeship to learn the precise steps and positions for the performance.

The dancers perform evocative titles like 'Dance of the Lords of Cremation Grounds', 'Dance of the Terrifying Deities', etc. While members of the community perform folk dances and music, the *Cham* are performances by monks who regard the performance as a spiritual practice.

Ritual music is played using cymbal, drum, flute, and yak-horn to accompany the dances. Dancers usually wear wooden masks that represent animals and fearsome deities. The *tshechu* festival held over several days often ends with a dance dedicated to the eight manifestations of Guru Rinpoche. The most distinctive mask represents the wrathful manifestation of Guru Rinpoche, which he transformed into to tame harmful deities.

Each dancer visualise their body as a divine being

The dances re-enact the events that took place during the life of Padmasambhava, mostly depicting goodness triumphing over evil. The Bhutanese believe that just by observing the sacred dances, they will be blessed, enlightened and purified.

Each dance performance requires meticulous efforts

The Atsara is a cultural icon

Several Atsaras provide comic relief at the annual festivals

Atsaras

The Atsara — a comical character in a red mask and a big phallus on top of his head — plays a vital role in Bhutanese festivals. These humorous figures are often associated with clowns due to their wittiness and burlesque appearance at tshechus. However, these Atsara figures are more than clowns for entertainment. The Atsara holds the responsibility of being the master of ceremony to ensure that the festival runs smoothly and, more importantly, helps the audience put their worries behind. In modern times, the Atsara also plays the role of an advocate to educate the masses on important issues such as personal well-being and hygiene.

The term 'Atsara' originated from the Sanskrit word acārya (holy Indian masters). Thus, we can say that the Atsara is a teacher who reminds the audience to let go of their inhibitions and unleash their free spirit. 🙰🙰

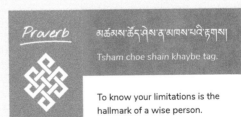

Proverb

 མཚམས་ཆོད་ཤེས་ན་མཁས་པའི་རྟགས།

Tsham choe shain khaybe tag.

To know your limitations is the hallmark of a wise person.

The Unfurling of a *Thongdrel*

Thongdrel means 'liberation at sight'. The final act of any *tshechu* festival is the unfurling of a *thongdrel*, a huge appliqué *thangka* often the size of a wall at a monastery. These giant religious scrolls depicting images of Guru Rinpoche and various spiritual deities are so sacred that Bhutanese believe the mere sight of it can purify obstacles and help them accumulate great merits. Typically, the Bhutanese unfurl the *thongdrel* at an early hour in the morning — around 3 to 4am — and roll it up by 7.30am to avoid direct sunlight on the *thongdrel*.

Bhutanese seek blessings from a silk appliqué *throngdel* of Guru Rinpoche at the end of a festival

Trekking
in Bhutan

In eastern Bhutan, traditional Bhutanese houses are built with stones

Trails in Bhutan

Bhutan is home to some of the most magnificent Himalayan trails, including the most challenging high-altitude treks in the world. The mountains of Bhutan offer unspoiled and uncrowded wilderness experiences with incredible views of the Himalayan peaks. Trekking in Bhutan is also one of the most exciting and unforgettable ways to experience the kingdom.

Whether you are an experienced hiker or a novice, you will find trails in Bhutan that suit your fitness level.

Bhutan offers treks of various durations. There are short treks ranging from a few days to month-long expeditions.

The kingdom is also in the midst of reviving an ancient trail formerly used by armies and traders for thousands of years. Soon, you'll be able to embark on the Trans Bhutan Trail, an exhilarating long-distance trail traversing mountain ridges, lush valleys and dozens of quaint towns and villages.

For more information, check out **www.bhutantreks.com.**

Trekking Season

Jan	Feb	Mar	Apr	May	Jun	Jul	Aug	Sep	Oct	Nov	Dec
		Bumdra Trek (7 days)						Bumdra Trek (7 days)			
		Jomolhari Trek (7 or 11 days)									
		Druk Path (9 days)									
		Dagala Thousand Lakes Trek (9 days)									
		Rodung La Trek (9 days)									
					Salt Trek (9 days)						
		Royal Manas Trek (10 days)						Royal Manas Trek (10 days)			
		Samtengang Trek (11 days)									
		Merak-Sakteng Trek (18 days)						Merak-Sakteng Trek (18 days)			
		Laya-Gasa Trek (21 days)									
			Lunana Snowman Trek (28 days)								
*Between mid-June and mid-September, you should expect regular rainfall.											

Difficulty level

⬤ Average   ⬤ High   ⬤ **Ultra High**

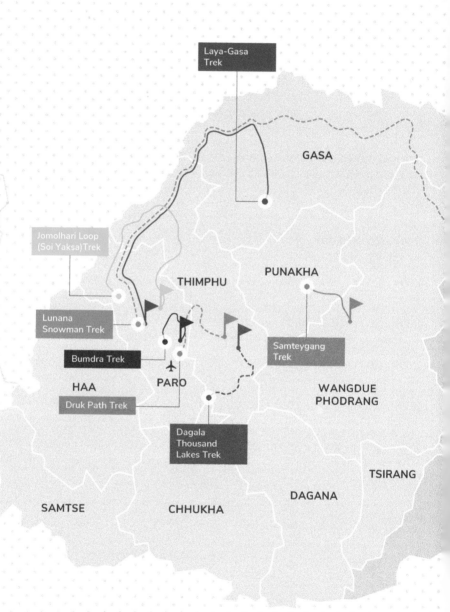

Laya-Gasa Trek

GASA

Jomolhari Loop (Soi Yaksa)Trek

THIMPHU

PUNAKHA

Lunana Snowman Trek

Bumdra Trek

Samteygang Trek

HAA

PARO

WANGDUE PHODRANG

Druk Path Trek

Dagala Thousand Lakes Trek

SAMTSE

CHHUKHA

DAGANA

TSIRANG

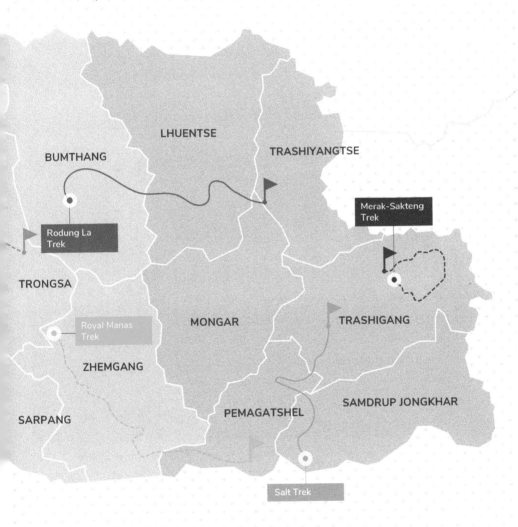

Bhutan Trekking Map

- ● Start
- ⚑ End
- ⚏ Trails
- ✈ Paro Airport

TIBET (AUTONOMOUS REGION OF CHINA)

LHUENTSE

BUMTHANG

TRASHIYANGTSE

Rodung La Trek

Merak-Sakteng Trek

TRONGSA

Royal Manas Trek

MONGAR

TRASHIGANG

ZHEMGANG

SARPANG

PEMAGATSHEL

SAMDRUP JONGKHAR

Salt Trek

INDIA

Bumdra Trek

7 DAYS

Difficulty level:	**Moderate**
Max elevation:	**3,900 m**
Min elevation:	**2,800 m**
Season:	**Feb to May, Sep to Nov**
Start from:	**Sang Choekor**
End at:	**Ramthangkha**

Huddle around a bonfire at night with your camping buddies for memories that'll last you a lifetime

Bumdra Trek, also known as 'Trek of Thousand Dakinis', is Bhutan's most beautiful short-duration trek, with one night of camping in the wilderness. It's the ideal trek if you love nature yet do not have much time in Bhutan. The views and sceneries along the way are breathtaking. You will also get a spectacular view of the iconic landmark of Bhutan — Taktsang Monastery, aka Tiger's Nest Monastery — from the top!

Highlights

- Sightseeing in Thimphu, Punakha and Paro
- Visit Sang Choekhor Shedra, a Buddhist college
- Visit the iconic Taktsang Monastery (Tiger's Nest Monastery)

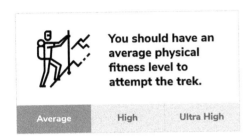

You should have an **average physical fitness level to attempt the trek.**

| Average | High | Ultra High |

PARO

THIMPHU

Bumdra Trek

HAA

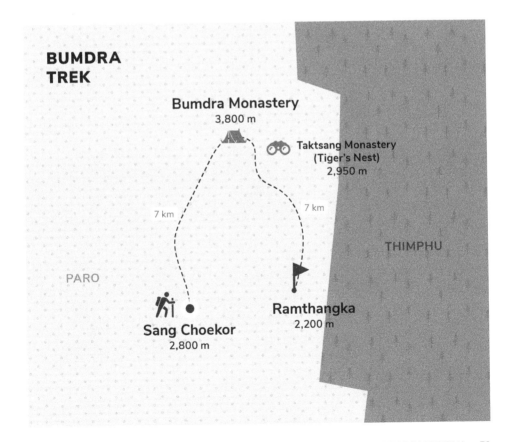

BUMDRA TREK

Bumdra Monastery
3,800 m

Taktsang Monastery (Tiger's Nest)
2,950 m

7 km

7 km

THIMPHU

PARO

Sang Choekor
2,800 m

Ramthangka
2,200 m

Camp overnight in the wilderness while enjoying the view of the spectacular mountains

Dagala Thousand Lakes Trek

9 DAYS

Difficulty level:	**Moderate**
Max elevation:	**4,720 m**
Min elevation:	**2,250 m**
Season:	**March to October**
Start from:	**Geynikha Village**
End at:	**Chamgang**

Stunning views of the Himalayan mountains and pristine lakes

The trek begins in Geynikha village and takes you through pristine and crystal-clear lakes. You will see exquisite wildflowers and gaze at the spectacular Himalayan range. Expect to see mountains like Mt Everest, Mt Jomolhari, Masang Gang, Jichu Drake, and Gangche Ta. You will also traverse through several quaint Bhutanese villages and experience an authentic village lifestyle.

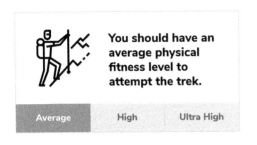

You should have an average physical fitness level to attempt the trek.

| Average | High | Ultra High |

THIMPHU   PUNAKHA

PARO

Dagala Thousand Lakes Trek

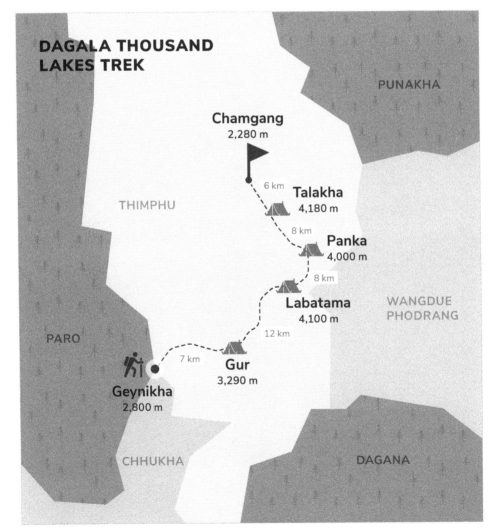

DAGALA THOUSAND LAKES TREK

PUNAKHA

Chamgang
2,280 m

6 km

Talakha
4,180 m

THIMPHU

8 km

Panka
4,000 m

8 km

Labatama
4,100 m

WANGDUE
PHODRANG

12 km

PARO

7 km

Gur
3,290 m

Geynikha
2,800 m

CHHUKHA

DAGANA

Highlights

- Hike through an ancient trail that was once an important trade route connecting Thimphu and Dagana
- Catch a sight of the breathtaking peaks of Mt Everest, Mt Jomolhari, and Mt Jichu Drake
- Hike through pristine alpine lakes, high yak pastures and beautiful meadows
- Traverse through mountain villages of Gur, Labatama, and Panka
- Experience the unique local semi-nomadic lifestyle
- Discover some of the most sacred Buddhist monasteries
- Visit the iconic Taktsang Monastery (Tiger's Nest Monastery)

Dagala Thousand Lakes Trek takes you by many small beautiful lakes

Jomolhari Loop Trek

7 OR 11 DAYS

Difficulty level:	**Moderate to Difficult**
Max elevation:	**5,000 m**
Min elevation:	**2,500 m**
Season:	**March to October**
Start from:	**Sharna Zampa**
End at:	**Gunitsawa**

Magnificent view of the Himalayan mountains

Jomolhari Loop Trek, also known as Soi Yaksa Trek, is one of Bhutan's most popular medium-level treks. Do not confuse it with the extended main Jomolhari Trek. It's the perfect trek for avid hikers who want to soak up the diverse landscapes of Bhutan. The altitude of Jomolhari Loop Trek ranges from 2,500 m to around 5,000 m. You can expect to see a wide variety of flora and fauna. Embark on Jomolhari Loop Trek for a fantastic panoramic view of the majestic Mount Jomolhari.

A fairly high level of fitness is required to complete the trek.

| Average | High | Ultra High |

PUNAKHA

PARO

THIMPHU

HAA

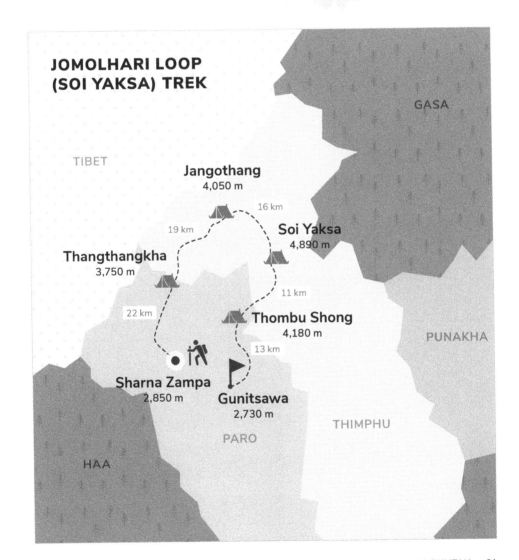

JOMOLHARI LOOP (SOI YAKSA) TREK

GASA

TIBET

Jangothang
4,050 m

16 km

19 km

Soi Yaksa
4,890 m

Thangthangkha
3,750 m

22 km

11 km

Thombu Shong
4,180 m

PUNAKHA

13 km

Sharna Zampa
2,850 m

Gunitsawa
2,730 m

HAA

PARO

THIMPHU

Highlights

- Experience astounding views of snow-capped mountains such as Mt Jomolhari and Mt Jichu Drake
- Traverse a variety of spectacular landscapes; enjoy the local flora and fauna
- Camp at the base of the sacred Mt Jomolhari
- Encounter wildlife such as blue sheep, marmots and the elusive snow leopards
- Discover Bhutan's unique culture with farmhouse visits
- Visit the iconic Taktsang Monastery (Tiger's Nest Monastery)

Stunning scenery and night view from the campsite

Merak-Sakteng Trek

18 DAYS

Difficulty level:	**Moderate to Difficult**
Max elevation:	**4,100 m**
Min elevation:	**1,500 m**
Season:	**Mar to May, Sep to Nov**
Start from:	**Chaling**
End at:	**Phongmey**

The lush green valleys of eastern Bhutan

The Merak-Sakteng Trek will take you to explore the nomadic areas of Bhutan. Unlike in the past, a new farm road now connects Merak to Sakteng. The trek is for adventurous souls who would like to explore the remote far east regions of the country.

The exotic valleys of Merak and Sakteng have been home to the indigenous tribes, the Brokpas, for centuries since their displacement from Tibet. The distinctive customs and lifestyle of the Brokpas make Merak and Sakteng rewarding places to explore. You will see Brokpas in attires and homes made out of yak hair!

A fairly high level of fitness is required to complete the trek.

Average	High	Ultra High

MERAK-SAKTENG TREK

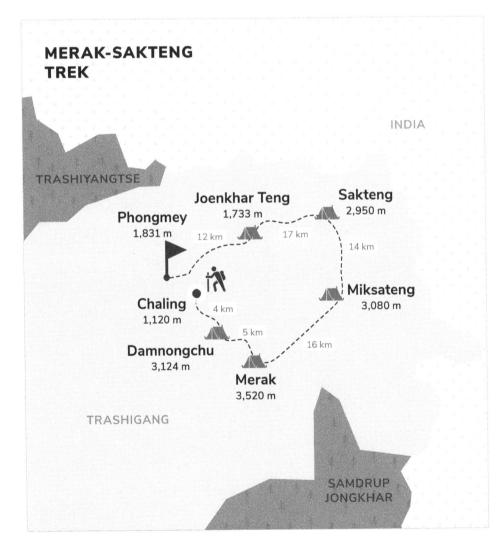

INDIA

TRASHIYANGTSE

Phongmey
1,831 m

Joenkhar Teng
1,733 m

12 km

17 km

Sakteng
2,950 m

14 km

Chaling
1,120 m

4 km

Miksateng
3,080 m

Damnongchu
3,124 m

5 km

16 km

Merak
3,520 m

TRASHIGANG

SAMDRUP JONGKHAR

Highlights

- Explore the Sakteng Wildlife Sanctuary, home to endangered animals, as well as the elusive and mythical yetis — locally known as *migois*
- Immerse in the rich biodiversity of Bhutan
- Hike through the Bumthang district, the spiritual heartland of Bhutan
- Explore eastern Bhutan's most scenic, pastoral valleys and remote villages
- Experience the unique lifestyle, culture, and tradition of the Brokpas
- Visit the iconic Taktsang Monastery (Tiger's Nest Monastery)

Most of the highlanders in Bhutan are yak herders

Lunana Snowman Trek

Difficulty level:	**Challenging**
Max elevation:	**5,320 m**
Min elevation:	**2,850 m**
Season:	**May to October**
Start from:	**Drukgyel Dzong**
End at:	**Sephu**

The indigenous Layaps in their traditional dress with their iconic conical hat

Snowman Trek is one of the most challenging treks in the world due to its high altitude, duration and distance, but it is also one of the most rewarding and beautiful treks in the Himalayas. The trail covers a distance of 230 km with an extreme elevation gain of 3,140 m. It goes through many steep ascents and descents.

Snowman Trek is the longest, remotest and undoubtedly most epic trek in the Himalayas. You will cross twelve mountain passes from 4,500 m to over 5,000 m. This demanding trek will bring you on a spectacular journey through Laya and Lunana. You'll encounter some of the world's rarest wildlife along the trek, such as the snow leopards.

Completing the Snowman Trek is truly an achievement to boast of as more people are climbing Mount Everest than those finishing the Snowman Trek!

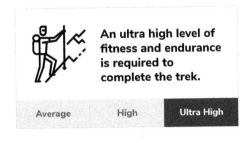

An ultra high level of fitness and endurance is required to complete the trek.

| Average | High | **Ultra High** |

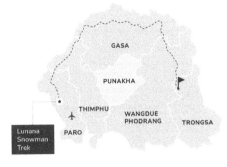

GASA

PUNAKHA

THIMPHU

WANGDUE
PHODRANG

TRONGSA

PARO

Lunana
Snowman
Trek

LUNANA SNOWMAN TREK

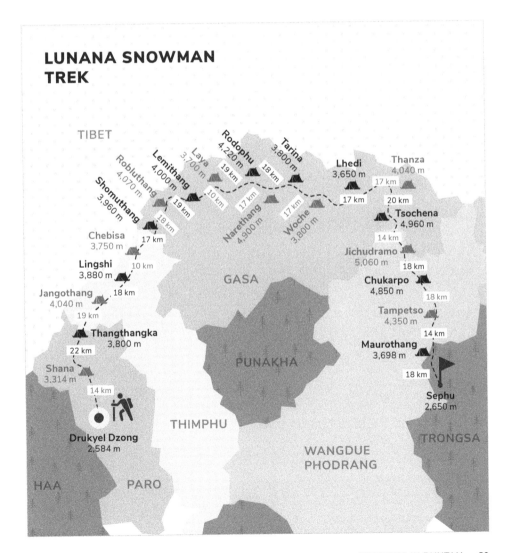

TIBET

Robluthang 4,070 m

Shomuthang 3,960 m

Lemithang 4,000 m — 19 km — Laya 3,700 m — 10 km — Rodophu 4,220 m — 18 km — Tarina 3,800 m — 17 km — Lhedi 3,650 m — 17 km — Thanza 4,040 m

19 km

18 km

Narethang 4,900 m — 17 km — Woche 3,800 m

Chebisa 3,750 m — 17 km

Lingshi 3,880 m — 10 km

Jangothang 4,040 m — 18 km

19 km

Thangthangka 3,800 m

22 km

Shana 3,314 m

14 km

Drukyel Dzong 2,584 m

GASA

PUNAKHA

THIMPHU

HAA

PARO

17 km — Thanza 4,040 m
20 km

Tsochena 4,960 m

14 km

Jichudramo 5,060 m — 18 km

Chukarpo 4,850 m

18 km

Tampetso 4,350 m

14 km

Maurothang 3,698 m

18 km

Sephu 2,650 m

WANGDUE
PHODRANG

TRONGSA

Highlights

- Cross twelve high mountain passes
- Explore the isolated Laya community and Bhutan's most remote region of Lunana
- Traverse beautiful landscapes, from lush valleys and dense forests to high mountain passes
- Get rewarded with spectacular views of Mt Jomolhari, Mt Jichu Drake, Masangang, Tiger Mountain, and Gangkar Puensum
- Soak in the Gasa Hot Springs to rejuvenate your body
- Explore and interact with the friendly yak herders
- Experience the unique cultures of the semi-nomadic tribes in Laya and Lunana
- Visit the iconic Taktsang Monastery (Tiger's Nest Monastery)

You'll see Bhutanese women threshing wheat using flails

Admire the breathtaking views of the Himalayan mountains by embarking on a trek

Travel
Tips

Part of the thrill of travelling is in
the planning. This section brings
you essential travel tips and
recommendations as you prepare
for your journey to Bhutan.

Travelling to Bhutan

Travel by Air

There is currently only one international airport in Bhutan, and it's located in the Paro district. You can only book flights to Bhutan through the national airline, Royal Bhutan Airlines, known as Drukair, or the privately owned Tashi Airlines, known as Bhutan Airlines.

Drukair flies to Bhutan from:
- Bangkok (Thailand)
- Singapore
- Kathmandu (Nepal)
- Dhaka (Bangladesh)
- New Delhi, Kolkata, Gaya, Bagdogra, and Guwahati (India)

Bhutan Airlines flies to Bhutan from:
- Bangkok (Thailand)
- Kathmandu (Nepal)
- Delhi (India)

Paro Airport has an extremely narrow runway

If you are planning a trip to Bhutan, you are highly encouraged to go through a tour operator, although it's not compulsory, as it will save you plenty of time! A tour operator is able to assist you with end-to-end the planning of your trip.

Book your trip **at least four to six months in advance,** especially if you plan to travel during the peak seasons of spring (February to May) or autumn (September to November). There are limited scheduled flights, and flights are restricted to daylight hours due to the difficulties in navigating the terrains. Hence, you should avoid a tight connecting flight.

Paro International Airport

With mountains as high as 5,000 m surrounding the airport and a narrow landing strip that is 2,265 m long and visible only moments before landing, it is no surprise that Paro Airport is deemed one of the most dangerous airports to land in. Other airports rely on the ILS (Instrument Landing System) to guide the aircraft laterally and vertically in an approach to land. On the other hand, the pilots only have one VOR (Very high-frequency Omni-directional Range) to guide them at Paro Airport. Most airports offer at least 18 km (10 nautical miles) of distance for pilots to gauge an aligned approach onto the landing strip, but Paro Airport accords only 1.8 km to 3.7 km (one to two nautical miles). All the factors above demand for the pilots to be very precise in landing. Thus only a handful of highly experienced pilots are qualified to land in Paro Airport.

Check out **www.paroairport.com** for the latest flight schedules.

Your tour operator will arrange for your tour guide to receive you at the airport if you book your trip through a tour operator.

If you have limited time in Bhutan, you can consider taking a domestic flight to reduce travel time. There are three domestic airports in Bhutan:

- Bathpalathang Airport (Bumthang)
- Gelephu Airport (Sarpang)
- Yonphulla Aiport (Trashigang)

Spectacular Himalayan mountains surround the Paro Airport

Travel by Land

You can also travel to Bhutan by land through the border towns via Phuentsholing, Samdrup Jongkhar or Gelephu.

Phuentsholing is located in southern Bhutan and is connected to the town of Jaigaon in India. It will take approximately six hours to drive 180 km from Phuentsholing to Bhutan's capital, Thimphu.

You can also enter via land from Samdrup Jongkhar in eastern Bhutan through the state of Assam in India. The journey from Guwahati Airport in India will take about three hours to reach Samdrup Jongkhar. Travellers usually enter through the Samdrup Jongkhar gateway if they intend to explore the districts in eastern Bhutan such as Trashigang, Trashiyangtse, Mongar or Lhuentse.

Gelephu is another entry point bordering the state of West Bengal in India. You will have to traverse across three districts to reach Thimphu. The travel time will take approximately ten hours.

Drukair at the runway of Paro Airport with the magnificent Paro Dzong in the background

Keep a lookout for all the tongue-in-cheek road signs in Bhutan

Bring along your medications if you are prone to motion sickness as the roads can be very winding

When should you visit Bhutan?

"

Aside from the weather patterns, something to consider when planning a trip to Bhutan is the festival schedule. Festivals are great opportunties to immerse in the local culture.

"

Spring (Mar - May)

High season

Spring is the popular season for tourists to visit Bhutan as the weather is ideal, and it's an excellent time for trekking. The valleys are green and lush as spring brings new growth with rhododendron, wild azaleas and wildflowers blooming from March to May.

Spring recommendations:

- Paro Tshechu in Paro (early April)
- Gomkora Festival in Trashigang (April)
- Savour the beautiful jacaranda blossoms at Punakha Dzong (April and May)
- Jomolhari Trek & Bumdra Trek (mid-April till end-May)

Tips

We highly recommend that you book your trip in advance. Flight tickets and hotels for the spring season are usually fully booked as early as January.

Experience the vibrant sacred dances of Bhutan

Paro Tshechu

Paro Tshechu is the most popular religious festival in Bhutan. This significant festival has been held annually since the 17th century when Zhabdrung Ngawang Namgyel and Ponpo Rigzin Nyingpo initiated the festival in conjunction with the consecration of Paro Dzong in 1644. Paro Tshechu is held for five days, and attending one will give you a great understanding of Bhutan's rich culture and history.

Check out
Paro Tshechu

s.bn.sg/parofest

Each dance performance has a story or special meaning behind it

The sacred Black Hat Dance where monks subdue demons with their spinning trance performance

Summer (Jun - Aug)

Low season

Although monsoon season starts in June and continues until August, Bhutan usually experiences only light showers in the afternoon. Occasionally, some drizzles last the entire day. Summer is the best time to visit Bhutan if you would like a closer and clearer view of the Himalayan mountains and to indulge in the lush green paddy fields. With lesser crowds during the summer, you can better soak in the atmosphere at the different attractions. With the days being longer in summer, you will also get to explore more places than you would during other seasons.

Summer recommendations:

- Nimalung Tshechu in Bumthang (June)
- Kurjey Tshechu in Bumthang (June)
- Haa Summer Festival in Haa (July)
- Masutake Mushroom Festival in Thimphu (August)

Nimalung Tshechu

Nimalung Tshechu is a 3-day festival held in Nimalung Buddhist Monastery in central Bhutan. It begins with the usual Cham performances. On the final day, visitors are blessed with the display of Guru Tshengye *thongdrel*.

The sound of the drums symbolises that Buddhism itself has no visible form

Drametse Ngacham is a sacred masked dance of the drums that originated from eastern Bhutan 500 years ago

Autumn (Sep - Nov)

High season

Just like spring, autumn is also a peak season for Bhutan due to the pleasantly mild weather with clear and crisp blue skies. It is one of the best times for trekking too as the climate is cool and temperate. You may look forward to basking in rice fields as they turn gold before the harvest.

Autumn recommendations:

- Thimphu Tshechu in Thimphu (September)
- Jakar Tshechu in Bumthang (October)
- Jambay Lhakhang Drup & Prakar Tshechu in Bumthang (November)
- Black-necked Crane Festival in Phobjikha Valley (11 November)

A play that depicts the Buddhist philosophy that everything is impermanent

Thimphu Tshechu

The 3-day festival gathers the largest audience of all the festivals in Bhutan. The tshechu is preceded by days and nights of prayers and rituals to invoke the gods. Monks prepare themselves with meditation and prayer for weeks ahead of the festival. The carnival-like atmosphere is a great opportunity for you to learn about Bhutan's rich cultural traditions.

The Black Hat Dance represents the tantric ritual of slaying the unruly demonic forces

Winter (Dec - Feb)

Low season

Winter is the best time for an exclusive experience on a snowy landscape in Bhutan. The weather can be cold in December, but the lowest temperature often occurs near the end of January. The higher regions usually experience snowfall. Heavy snowfall may cause some of the roads to central or eastern Bhutan to be impassable. If you would like to experience a less crowded Bhutan, winter is the time to visit as there are fewer tourists during this season. If you are lucky, you might even experience snowfall during your hike up to Taktsang Monastery (Tiger's Nest Monastery).

Winter recommendations:
- Druk Wangyel Tshechu (13 December)
- Trongsa Tshechu (December)
- Punakha Dromche & Tshechu (February)

Druk Wangyel Tshechu

Druk Wangyel Tshechu, established in 2011, is a special festival held as a tribute to the wise leadership of the fourth King, Jigme Singye Wangchuck and the armed forces' victory against the Assamese insurgents. Unlike the other festivals, the Royal Bhutan Army performs the dances during the festival instead of monks or commoners.

Check out Druk Wangyel Tshechu

s.bn.sg/dochulafest

The performances at Druk Wangyel Tshechu differ from the other tshechu festivals

One of the dances depicts five old men and women bestowing longevity and prosperity on the audience

Dancers portray celestial beings who bless and wish benefit upon all those in attendance

How much does it cost to travel to Bhutan?

Bhutan adheres to a strict 'High value, Low volume' tourism policy to avoid the effects of mass tourism. Since the beginning of tourism in Bhutan, the government has implemented an all-inclusive tour package for all tourists visiting the country. In the past, tourists paid a fixed Minimum Daily Package Rate (MDPR) ranging from USD200 to USD290 per person per night, depending on the season of their visit and the number of travellers. USD65 of the MDPR was paid to the government as a Sustainable Development Fee (SDF), and the remainder was used for lodging, transportation, meals, driver and tour guide.

However, the COVID-19 pandemic has forced the country to review its decades-long 'High value, Low volume' tourism policy. To prevent the negative effects of mass tourism in Bhutan, the government realised that it has to tighten its doors further and redefine the meaning of 'high value, low volume'.

Hence, a new tourism levy bill was passed in June 2022 to increase the Sustainable Development Fee (SDF) to USD200 per person per night. Regional tourists from India, Maldives and Bangladesh are required to pay the SDF of Nu. 1200 (~USD15) per person per night.

With the increased SDF, the government aims to improve Bhutan's tourism infrastructure and focus on long-term sustainability. The kingdom hope to achieve less carbon footprint and greater quality of tourist experience in the long run. In short, Bhutan wants to reap maximum benefits for both visitors and the locals.

In addition to the increased SDF, visitors are now required to pay an entrance fee ranging from Nu. 1000 (~USD12.50) to Nu. 2000 (~USD25) when visiting various national monuments or sacred sites.

Approximate cost of travelling to Bhutan

A complete tour inclusive of SDF, standard hotel, tour guide, transportation and meals will cost approximately:

- **3 pax or more:** USD300 to USD400 per person per day

- **2 pax:** USD350 to USD450 per person per day

- **Solo:** USD400 to USD480 per day

Above are just rough estimations as much of it will depend on the choice of accommodation, activities and engagement of a guide or a driver. If you plan to visit just the major cities like Thimphu and Paro for sightseeing without any tour guide and travel by local taxi, the price might be reduced slightly.

The tour guides in Bhutan are knowledgeable and extremely friendly, don't hesitate to ask them questions

Do children have to pay the full cost?

Children below the age of 5 are exempted from the Sustainable Development Fee. Children aged 5 to 12 years old are only required to pay USD100 per person per night. However, the visa application fee of USD40 is still applicable for all. The previous student concession rate is no longer applicable under the new tourism policy.

Can I travel to Bhutan as a solo traveller or business traveller?

Yes. Bhutan welcomes all travellers: solo backpackers, group travellers, and corporate groups, including those who are travelling for meetings, incentives, conferences and exhibition (MICE) purposes. Your tour operator (if any) or sponsoring entity in Bhutan will assist you to apply for the appropriate visa and permits.

How much is the visa application fee?

All tourists (except regional tourists) require a visa before travelling to Bhutan. The visa application fee costs USD40. You can apply for the visa online at www.bhutantravel/visa, or if you're travelling with a tour operator, or staying at a hotel, they can also apply for the visa on your behalf. It will take approximately five working days for the submission review.

Do I need to purchase travel insurance?

While travel insurance is not compulsory, it is always advisable to purchase travel insurance when travelling to protect yourself from any losses that may arise due to unexpected or unforeseen circumstances. If you do not have any existing travel insurance, your tour operator should be able to purchase travel insurance on your behalf or refer you to an insurer.

Accommodation recommendations

Bhutan has strict rules and regulations for hotel management within the country. Tourism Council of Bhutan (TCB) evaluates each hotel to ensure that the properties meet the standard and criteria required. Only those with a 3-star rating and above can host international tourists. Hence, as a tourist, you can have a peace of mind that your accommodations in Bhutan will be satisfying and comfortable.

Popular Standard Tourist Hotels

Paro
Tashi Namgay Resort
Metta Resort
Rema Resort
Tenzinling Resort

Thimphu
Namgay Heritage
Khang Residency
Hotel Osel

Punakha
Hotel Lobesa
The Four Boutique Hotel

Gangtey
Dewachen Hotel
ABC Lodge

Bumthang
Valley Resort
Rinchenling Lodge

Mongar
Wangchuk Hotel

Trashigang
Druk Deothjung Hotel

Top Luxury Hotels

COMO Uma
Locations: Paro, Punakha

COMO Uma is an ideal accommodation if you are looking for a deluxe stay. COMO Hotels and Resorts offer luxury travel experiences with personalised service in elegant properties, each individually curated to reflect its location.

The luxury rooms combine colourful accents of traditional Bhutanese craftsmanship with the clean-lined contemporary design for which COMO Hotels and Resorts are known.

One of COMO Uma Paro Hotel's most exciting events was in 2008 when Hong Kong superstars Tony Leung and Carina Lau held their wedding party on-site. The Bukhari restaurant at COMO Uma Paro is also a royal favourite.

Meanwhile, COMO Uma Punakha, an intimate luxury lodge, earned its title as the #1 Resort in Asia: Condé Nast Traveller Readers' Choice Awards from 2017 to 2020. The hotel is located in the far western end of the picturesque Punakha valley overlooking a snake-like bend in the Mo Chhu river.

COMO Uma Punakha Valley View Room

Amankora

Locations: Paro, Thimphu, Punakha, Gangtey, Bumthang

The first resort in Bhutan with five lodges across its central and western valleys, Amankora has been part of this legendary Buddhist kingdom for 17 years. Amankora's five lodges are sanctuaries designed to complement its uniquely beautiful setting.

Aman is one of the iconic brands to have emerged from Asia, dedicated to providing an unparalleled experience. Widely acclaimed as one of the best luxury resort brands globally, Aman is known for premium service and luxury, high profile clientele and the most exotic locations. 'Aman' means 'peace' in Sanskrit, and 'kora' means 'circumambulate' in Dzongkha.

Surrounded by forests and orchards, the five lodges comprise 76 suites that fuse rustic elements with contemporary design. There is no television in the rooms, though you probably don't need it given the stunning views surrounding the lodges.

Each lodge organises different activities in the evening. You can enjoy cultural programmes with traditional Bhutanese dances at the Thimphu and Punakha lodges.

Amankora Punakha Suite

Le Méridien
Locations: Paro, Thimphu

Le Méridien is an upper-upscale, design-focused international hotel brand with a European perspective.

Located at the heart of Bhutan's capital city, Le Méridien Thimphu is just steps away from shops and entertainment. It is conveniently accessible to popular attractions such as National Memorial Chorten, Tashichho Dzong, and Thimphu town.

The hotel provides an excellent mix of local and international cuisine. They have a Pan-Asian restaurant that serves authentic South-East Asian flavours.

Meanwhile, Le Méridien Paro, Riverfront is the largest five-star hotel in Paro with the highest room inventory in the area. Located just 10 minutes away from Paro Airport, the resort is situated on the edge of the Paro River, offering panoramic views of the eastern Himalayas.

The resort in Paro is a popular choice for international business travellers as it has the most outstanding meeting spaces in the kingdom.

Le Méridien Paro Grand Deluxe Room

Six Senses

Locations: Paro, Thimphu, Punakha, Gangtey, Bumthang

Six Senses is a luxury brand renowned for its focus on wellness and sustainability. The five Six Senses Bhutan lodges have been thoughtfully designed to fully immerse travellers in the kingdom's natural beauty and culture, offering a contemporary take on traditional Bhutanese architecture and form. The lodges, which vary in style from valley to valley, showcase each location's diversity and special character. The properties range in size and facilities, but all of Six Senses properties are focused on sustainability practices, echoing the values of Bhutan.

Six Senses Punakha, also known as 'The Flying Farmhouse Amidst the Rice Fields', is the most popular lodge. This spectacular lodge has a more rustic rural feel, complementing the warmer climate it's in while offering sweeping views of the valley filled with rice paddy fields and dotted with traditional farmhouses.

A highlight of Six Senses Punakha is the crescent-shaped outdoor infinity pool overlooking the stunning Punakha valley.

Six Senses Paro Lodge Suite

Other Boutique and Luxury Hotels in Bhutan

Bhutan Spirit Sanctuary
Location: Paro

Gangtey Lodge
Location: Phobjikha Valley (Gangtey)

Naksel Boutique
Location: Paro

Norkhil Boutique Hotel
Location: Thimphu

Zhiwa Ling Ascent
Location: Thimphu

Taj Tashi
Location: Thimphu

Terma Linca Resort
Location: Thimphu

The Pema by Realm
Location: Thimphu

The Postcard Dewa
Location: Thimphu

Zhiwa Ling Heritage
Location: Paro

Bhutan Spirit Sanctuary Terrace Room

Climate and Temperature

The climate in Bhutan varies due to its topography and differences in altitudes. Bhutan has three climatic zones: subtropical in the south, temperate in the middle and subalpine in the north.

Climatic Zones of Bhutan

Northern Zone

The northern zone has a harsher climate and is much colder during winter. Mountain peaks are perpetually covered in snow, and lower-lying areas are cool in summer.

Central Zone

The central zone has a seasonal climate with warm summers before the monsoon. The winters are usually cool and dry with clear blue skies.

Cold climate in northern Bhutan

Clear blue skies in central Bhutan

Temp in	°c	Jan	Feb	Mar	Apr	May	Jun	Jul	Aug	Sep	Oct	Nov	Dec
Paro west	max	9.4	13.4	14.5	17.6	23.5	25.4	26.8	25.3	23.4	18.7	13.9	11.2
	min	-5.8	1.5	0.6	4.6	10.6	13.1	14.9	14.7	11.7	7.4	1.4	-1.7
Thimphu west	max	12.3	14.4	16.4	20.0	22.5	24.4	18.9	25.0	23.1	29.1	17.9	14.5
	min	-2.6	0.6	3.9	7.1	13.1	15.2	13.4	15.8	15.0	10.4	0.5	-1.1
Punakha west	max	16.1	19.6	21.2	24.4	27.2	31.2	32.0	31.4	29.9	27.8	22.3	15.0
	min	4.2	5.3	9.2	11.9	14.8	19.5	21.6	19.8	20.0	18.9	13.0	7.9
Wangdue west	max	17.0	19.0	22.8	26.2	29.9	29.2	18.4	29.1	27.5	26.1	22.6	19.1
	min	4.3	7.8	10.4	12.9	17.7	20.1	16.2	20.0	19.1	14.7	9.6	6.3
Trongsa central	max	13.0	13.9	16.7	20.1	21.0	22.2	25.3	23.8	22.6	21.8	19.8	18.2
	min	-0.2	0.4	4.4	6.6	11.6	13.6	15.3	15.0	14.2	11.7	6.4	2.5
Bumthang central	max	10.8	10.0	16.2	18.7	21.3	22.5	14.1	23.0	21.6	19.5	16.1	12.3
	min	-5.1	-1.4	3.5	3.9	9.5	13.5	10.9	13.7	12.1	5.9	-0.5	-2.3
Mongar east	max	15.5	15.9	20.0	22.8	25.1	26.1	27.1	25.4	24.7	22.7	19.9	17.7
	min	8.2	8.3	11.6	14.0	17.4	19.5	19.8	19.6	19.4	15.8	11.2	9.5
Trashigang east	max	20.4	21.7	24.8	28.3	30.0	30.7	31.5	30.2	30.0	29.1	26.1	23.0
	min	10.5	11.5	14.4	17.0	22.6	22.6	23.1	22.7	21.9	17.7	13.6	11.6

Humid weather in southern Bhutan

Southern Zone

The southern zone has a hot and humid subtropical climate with a monsoon season that is consistent throughout the year. The southern region also receives a significant amount of rain, and heavy rainfall can sometimes cause landslides and render roads impassable.

Places of Interest

Driving time between various places in Bhutan

From	To	Distance (km)	Time (Approx.)
Thimphu	Paro	54	1 hr
Thimphu	Phuentsholing	176	6 hrs
Thimphu	Wangdue Phodrang	70	2 hrs
Thimphu	Haa	114	4 hours
Thimphu	Phobjikha Valley (Gangtey)	135	4 hours 30 mins
Thimphu	Bumthang	270	8 hours 30 mins
Thimphu	Punakha	84	3 hours
Punakha	Wangdue Phodrang	23	45 min
Wangdue Phodrang	Trongsa	129	4 hrs 30 mins
Trongsa	Bumthang	68	2 hrs 30 mins
Bumthang	Mongar	193	7 hrs
Mongar	Lhuentse	75	2 hrs 30 mins
Mongar	Trashigang	91	3 hrs 30 mins
Trashigang	Trashiyangtse	55	1 hr 30 mins
Trashigang	Samdrup Jongkhar	180	6 hrs 30 mins

Thimphu

Western Bhutan

GASA

PUNAKHA

LHUENTSE

TRASHIYANGTSE

BUMTHANG

PARO

THIMPHU

WANGDUE PHODRANG

TRONGSA

HAA

MONGAR

TRASHIGANG

ZHEMGANG

DAGANA

TSIRANG

SARPANG

PEMAGATSHEL

SAMDRUP JONGKHAR

SAMTSE

CHHUKHA

Thimphu is the capital of Bhutan and the largest city in the country, located in the western region. It is also the political and economic hub of the country that houses most of the important government buildings and constitutional agencies. Many of the locals from rural places migrate to Thimphu to seek employment. This vibrant city contains a rustic charm that has much to offer to travellers. It is the seat of government of Bhutan, with an ancient dzong and a more recent House of Parliament nearby. You can also find many cafes and handicraft shops around Thimphu town.

Attractions

- Buddha Dordenma
- Tashichho Dzong
- Jungshi Handmade Paper Factory
- Royal Textile Academy
- Simply Bhutan
- Folk Heritage Museum
- Motithang Takin Preserve
- Bhutan Postal Museum
- National Memorial Chorten
- Simtokha Dzong
- Dochula Pass
- Druk Wangyal Lhakhang

Buddha Dordenma — a place for spiritual seekers and contemplation

Buddha Dordenma

Buddha Dordenma, also known as Buddha Point, is a famous attraction in Bhutan. This sitting Buddha statue that measures 51.5 m in height is one of the largest sitting Buddha statues in the world.

The Buddha Dordenma statue is made of solid bronze and gilded with paint, as are all of the 125,000 smaller Buddha statues placed within the giant statue; 100,000 of the statues are 8 inches tall, and 25,000 of the statues are 12 inches tall.

You can visit the majestic meditation hall with beautifully carved pillars painted in gold. There is also a gold statue of the four-faced Buddha inside the hall. Walls are elegantly painted with murals of various stories of the life of the Buddha.

From Buddha Point, you get an overview of the beautiful Thimphu city.

Tashichho Dzong

Tashichho Dzong, or commonly known as Thimphu Dzong, is an impressive structure situated in the northern part of Thimphu city that plays the dual role of housing the administration of the state and the clergy. Tashichho Dzong has been the seat of the government since 1952. It currently houses the throne room and offices of the King of Bhutan, the cabinet secretariat, and the ministries of home affairs and finance.

As a tourist, you will not be allowed to visit the offices in the dzong. But you can visit the monastery in the dzong, which is home to the Chief Abbot of Bhutan and a retinue of monks during most of the year. The

If you visit Bhutan between April to July, you may see a stretch of colourful rhododendron flowers greeting you along the pathway of the dzong. Alternatively, if you visit in March, you may also be in luck and see the blooming cherry trees!

clergy moves to the Punakha Dzong in the winter, where the climate is warmer.

You can explore the surroundings of the dzong and admire the marvellous architecture. Interestingly, you can also find a replica of the original Tashichho Dzong in Kagawa, Shikoku in Japan.

The much celebrated Thimphu Tshechu held at Tashichho Dzong attracts large crowds every autumn

Jungshi Handmade Paper Factory

Pay a visit to Jungshi Handmade Paper Factory to watch the making of authentic Bhutanese paper known as dey-sho. For many generations, Bhutanese practised the traditional method of producing dey-sho papers from the bark of the Daphne tree.

This ancient craft is one of the thirteen traditional arts of Bhutan that the country preserves. Bhutanese originally used dey-sho papers in monasteries for woodblock printing, manuscripts, and prayer books.

In the factory, you can also find other paper products like stationeries, greeting cards and journals that make unique souvenirs.

You can try your hand at this ancient craft and make some traditional papers of your own

Royal Textile Academy

Weaving is an integral part of Bhutanese culture and tradition. The Royal Textile Academy (RTA) is the first institution dedicated to preserving, promoting and educating people about Bhutanese textiles.

RTA is home to the only textile museum in Bhutan, where it hosts different textile exhibitions throughout the year.

Through RTA, you can learn about the textile heritage, different weaving styles, and the intricacies of handwoven textiles in Bhutan. Each district in Bhutan has a distinctive weaving style and patterns unique to them.

A visit to the textile museum will give you a better appreciation of the beautiful traditional dress, *kira* and *gho*, that you see the locals wear.

RTA showcases the intricate art of weaving at its Textile Museum

Folk Heritage Museum

The Folk Heritage Museum is set inside a three-storey 19th-century traditional house. The museum provides visitors with a glimpse of the traditional Bhutanese lifestyle and artefacts in a conventional household.

The museum perfectly recaptures the rural setting and ambience of a traditional household. There's a collection of household objects, tools and equipment found in a typical Bhutanese home with paddy, wheat and millet fields set up outdoors and a traditional water-mill with millstones that are more than 150 years old. There is a traditional kitchen and a hot stone bath that is famous on farmsteads throughout the country.

Visiting the museum will allow you to learn more about Bhutanese culture, customs and traditions.

Artisan Pema Tshering refined the art of woodcarving after studying at the Institute of Zorig Chusum, where Queen Mother Ashi Tshering Pem supported his education

Simply Bhutan

Simply Bhutan is an interactive museum that offers you an excellent guided introduction to different aspects of traditional Bhutanese life.

This is an excellent place for your induction into Bhutan. You will learn how to dress up in Bhutanese traditional dress, distil ara (rice wine), and understand how Bhutanese construct their homes out of rammed earth. At the museum, you can also enjoy some local butter tea while watching local dance performances.

The museum primarily is a unique example of ancient Bhutanese architecture. The museum's structure was built reusing old timber, door and window frames, and numerous other materials from demolished houses.

Unlike most museums where you cannot touch the artefacts or take photographs, you can snap away freely here. You can also try a hand at archery and the local dart game known as *khuru*.

At the museum, you'll get to meet Pema Tshering, a talented foot artist who has been diagnosed with cerebral palsy. There is a little shop inside Simply Bhutan where Pema does his wood carving and painting using his foot. If you see him, don't hesitate to say hello or support his artwork.

Do check out the inspiring story of Pema Tshering.

s.bn.sg/pematshering

Motithang Takin Preserve

Motithang Takin Preserve is a wildlife reserve for takins, the national animal of Bhutan. The mini zoo was converted into a preserve because the takins refrained from inhabiting the surrounding forest after they were set free.

Legend has it that the famous spiritual master, Drukpa Kuenley, also known as the 'Divine Madman', is responsible for creating this unique creature, a gnu goat that resembles an ox but is more closely related to a sheep.

One day during the 15th century, people in Bhutan asked Drukpa Kuenley to perform a miracle at the end of a feast. So, he took the head of a goat, fixed it to a cow's skeletons, and with a snap, created the takin.

Some claim that the takin is the most queer-looking animal that they have ever seen!

After visiting the Takin Preserve, ask your guide to bring you to the Bhutan Broadcasting Station (BBS) Tower. A five to ten minutes drive to the upper part of the road will lead to Sangaygang BBS Tower at 2,685 m. Colourful prayer flags are strung around the trees above the BBS Tower. From here, you'll get a picturesque photo background of the entire Thimphu city.

Discover one of nature's wonders — Bhutan's national animal, the Takin

Bhutan Postal Museum

The Bhutan Postal Museum is home to the world's largest photo book and most bizarre collection of Bhutanese stamps that will intrigue any philatelist. There are five galleries in the museum that trace the development of the Bhutanese postal system, from the earliest mail runners who delivered mail to the remotest villages to Bhutan's most unusual stamps. There are also historical reminders of the time when people still hand-wrote letters and stuck stamps on them to share news.

One of the most interesting things you can do in Bhutan is to get your own personalised legitimate stamps at the General Post Office for Nu. 500 (around USD7). It contains 12 stamps with a mix value of Nu. 30, Nu. 45 and Nu. 50.

Go ahead to pick up some postcards, send greetings, and share some Bhutanese love with your family and friends.

National Memorial Chorten

The National Memorial Chorten is a prominent stupa erected in 1974 in honour of the Father of Modern Bhutan, the third King, Jigme Dorji Wangchuck. The stupa is a famous landmark located in the heart of Thimphu city with its golden spire and bells.

The Memorial Chorten is designed in a classical style of stupas with a pyramidal pillar crowned by a crescent moon and sun. A distinctive feature of the chorten is the outward flaring of the rounded part, giving it a pyramidal shape instead of a dome shape.

Create your personalised stamps in Bhutan

The memorial chorten is a popular site for meditation

Simtokha Dzong

Simtokha Dzong is the first fortress to be built in the kingdom in the 17th century and the first building to incorporate monastic and administrative centres in Bhutan. The central tower is three-storey high, with prayer wheels surrounding the courtyard. An interesting feature of the dzong is that the courtyard has more than 300 slate carvings that depict Buddhist figures.

On top of being an important historical monument, it also houses one of Bhutan's top-ranking Dzongkha language institutes.

Visiting Simtokha Dzong will give you insights into Bhutan's early days when Zhabdrung Ngawang Namgyal first unified Bhutan nearly four centuries ago.

Do remember to circumambulate in a clockwise direction, as with any religious structure in Bhutan.

Simtokha Dzong has been restored to its former state through careful conservation

On a clear day, you can see a stunning panorama of the Himalayas from Dochula Pass

Dochula Pass

Dochula Pass is located between Thimphu and Punakha at an elevation of 3,100 m. There are two significant landmarks on this mountain pass; one is **Druk Wangyal Lhakhang** that was built to commemorate the centenary of monarchy in Bhutan.

The other is the **108 memorial stupas** built to honour the fourth King, Jigme Singye Wangchuck, for ensuring the sovereignty and security of the country when he led Bhutanese troops in 2003 to flush out Indian militants who camped on Bhutanese territory. Both monuments were built by the Queen Mother, Dorji Wangmo Wangchuck.

In commemoration of the occasion, the Dochula Druk Wangyal Festival is held annually on 13 December in an open area near the monastery.

The view from Dochula Pass is breathtaking. Weather permitting, you can even see the Himalayan mountains from the pass, including Gangkar Puensum, the highest unclimbed mountain in the world.

You can light butter lamps at Druk Wangyal Lhakhang

Punakha

Western Bhutan

GASA
PUNAKHA
PARO
THIMPHU
HAA
WANGDUE PHODRANG
LHUENTSE
TRASHIYANGTSE
BUMTHANG
TRONGSA
MONGAR
TRASHIGANG
DAGANA
TSIRANG
ZHEMGANG
SAMTSE
CHHUKHA
SARPANG
PEMAGATSHEL
SAMDRUP JONGKHAR

Once upon a time, Punakha used to be the capital of Bhutan. It was the seat of government until 1955 when the administration moved to Thimphu.

Punakha is also the main district for rice production in Bhutan.

Lush beautiful paddy fields and rice terraces will greet you as you enter Punakha. The pleasing landscapes and significant sites in the district make Punakha one of the most popular tourist destinations in the country.

Attractions

- Chimi Lhakhang
- Sopsokha Village
- Po Chhu Suspension Bridge
- Punakha Dzong
- Sangchhen Dorji Lhuendrup Nunnery
- Whitewater Rafting
- Khamsum Yulley Namgyal Chorten

Khamsum Yulley Namgyal Chorten

Take a morning hike to Khamsum Yulley Namgyal Chorten, a picturesque chorten built by the third Queen Mother, Tshering Yangdon Wangchuck. You can reach this charming monastery with just a one hour hike through the woods and paddy fields. The chorten is an example of magnificent Bhutanese architecture. The Queen Mother built this four-storey pagoda-style stupa to protect Bhutan and bring peace to all sentient beings and the world. It offers a spectacular view of the whole Punakha valley.

Bhutanese craftsmen took nine years to build this elegant and sacred piece of architecture

Sopsokha Village

Before you reach Chimi Lhakhang temple, you will usually begin your walk from Sopsokha village, where some traditional Bhutanese farmhouses have now turned into art and craft shops.

You can find phallic symbol souvenirs in all colours, shapes and sizes in some of these handicraft stores! While these phallic symbols can be seen flanking doorways, hanging off rooftops or painted on the walls of homes, you'll never find the phallic symbol on the walls of any temples or dzongs. The bizarre sight of phalluses wrapped in ribbons may surprise the uninitiated but the unusual symbol has a spiritual origin. You'll learn more about the fascinating tales associated with the symbol when you visit the famous Chimi Lhakhang.

From Sopsokha village, you'll take a pleasant 20-minute leisure stroll, passing through a large mustard and paddy field to reach the entrance of Chimi Lhakhang.

You'll find your pace naturally slowing down as you walk through the beautiful rice and mustard fields.

Sunset at the picturesque rice and mustard fields

Chimi Lhakhang

Chimi Lhakhang, also known as Chime Lhakhang or the Fertility Temple, is one of the highlights of a trip to Bhutan.

This sacred temple is associated with the famous spiritual adept, Drukpa Kuenley, the 'Divine Madman', a term used with respect and even fondness. He is known for his bizarre and unorthodox teachings that challenged preconceived notions of society. A celebrated persona in the Himalayas, Drukpa Kuenley used outrageous means and behaviour to expose hypocrisies in society, often aiming at the establishment, including the monastic community. Drukpa Kuenley is also associated with symbolic imagery such

as the phallus and has come to be described as a 'mad' saint that has spread the striking and creative symbol of the phallus all over the country — from souvenirs, wood sculptures to murals.

Chimi Lhakhang, built as a memorial to Drukpa Kuenley, is a popular pilgrimage site. Couples from all over the world and many Bhutanese who have trouble conceiving children visit the temple to pray in the belief that Drukpa Kuenley will bless them with children.

Check out **www.chimilhakhang.com** for heartwarming stories of couples who have successfully conceived after they visited and prayed at Chimi Lhakhang.

Chimi Lhakhang is a sacred temple in Bhutan, famous for fertility blessings

Pho Chhu
Suspension Bridge

If you're not afraid of heights, definitely check out the Punakha suspension bridge, the longest suspension bridge in Bhutan. It's the perfect spot for you to capture all your beautiful social media photos. The bridge measuring 160 m long is located above the broad and rapid Pho Chhu River. Traditionally, the bridge was constructed for the monks of Punakha Dzong to visit nearby villages.

Punakha Dzong

This magnificent dzong is the second-oldest and second-largest dzong in the country. It was also formerly named Pungtang Dechen Photrang Dzong, 'The Palace of Great Happiness'. Punakha Dzong is one of the top attractions in Bhutan due to its beautiful architecture and significant history. The building was the seat for the Royal Government of Bhutan before the capital relocated to Tashichho Dzong in Thimphu in 1955.

If you seek an adrenaline rush, walk across the Pho Chhu Suspension Bridge

The dzong sits majestically at the confluence between the Pho Chhu (*pho* refers to female) and Mo Chhu (*mo* refers to male) river.

The coronation of the first King, Ugyen Wangchuck, was held in Punakha Dzong in 1907. It was also the venue of the famed royal wedding ceremony of the King of Bhutan, Jigme Khesar Namgyel Wangchuck, and Queen Jetsun Pema in 2011.

Do check out the vibrant Punakha Tshechu

s.bn.sg/punakhafest

You may see beautiful jacarandas bloom in the courtyard of the dzong between April to May

Whitewater Rafting

If you are an adrenaline junkie or a thrill-seeker, consider whitewater rafting in Punakha. It's a fun activity to do with friends and family. You'll be rafting through the crystal-clear river, admiring the incredible landscapes of Punakha valley. No prior experience is required for the rafting as long as you do not mind getting a little wet by the end of it. All, including children aged 7 or the elderly, can enjoy whitewater rafting.

* Advanced booking required and charges apply.

Whitewater rafting is a safe activity carried out with highly trained and experienced rafting guides. The activity takes approximately two hours to complete. The best time for rafting is in March, April, and between November to December.

The rugged, untamed waterways of Bhutan will not disappoint the adventure-seekers

Sangchhen Dorji Lhuendrup Nunnery

Sangchhen Dorji Lhuendrup Nunnery overlooks the stunning Punakha and Wangdue Phodrang valleys from the courtyard. The nunnery was built to serve as a college to train nuns and currently houses about 120 nuns. The double-storey complex founded by Yab Ugyen Dorji — father of the Queen Mothers — showcases the finest craftsmanship in Bhutanese architecture, skilfully crafted by local artisans. The nunnery complex functions as a meditation centre and offers life-skills training to nuns: thangka painting, embroidery, tailoring and sculpting. The temple is also home to the tallest Avalokiteshvara statue in Bhutan; the statue is 4.2 m tall. There is also a striking chorten resembling Nepal's Boudhanath Stupa in the compound. You can immerse yourself in meditation sessions and observe the nuns' spiritual practice in the nunnery.

Sangchhen Dorji Lhuendrup Nunnery has a nice, quiet and peaceful ambience

Paro

Western Bhutan

Paro is the gateway to the kingdom where the international airport is located. Bhutan's most iconic landmark, Taktsang Monastery and many sacred sites and historic buildings are also located within Paro.

Paro has the perfect blend of ancient beauty and modern charm. It is one of the most vibrant and dynamic districts in Bhutan. In Paro town, you can find stretches of western-style cafés alongside traditional handicraft shops.

Attractions

- Taktsang Monastery
- Kyichu Lhakhang
- Tachog Lhakhang
- Jangtsa Dumtseg Lhakhang
- Dra Karpo
- Kila Goenpa
- Zuri Dzong
- Paro Dzong
- Drukgyel Dzong
- Dobji Dzong
- Namgay Artisanal Brewery
- Aum Choden Homestay
- Chencho Weaving House
- Chele La Pass

Taktsang Monastery (Tiger's Nest Monastery)

Popularly known as Tiger's Nest Monastery, this iconic landmark of Bhutan is no stranger to the world. A trip to Bhutan is incomplete without a visit to this majestic temple perched atop the cliffside about 900 m above Paro valley. Seeing this spectacular monastery with your own eyes will make you wonder how they accomplished this architectural feat in the 16th century!

The trek up and down Taktsang Monastery can take anywhere between 3.5 hours to 9 hours, depending on your fitness level. Throughout the climb, you will see many locals of all ages, including toddlers as young

It is advisable to start your trek early to avoid the afternoon heat. Remember to pack light and wear comfortable shoes for a smooth trekking experience. You can also rent a walking stick or hire a horse to take you up to the halfway point if needed. Above all, enjoy the stunning views and take plenty of photos.

as 2 years old, making their way up to the monastery. Parents carrying infants on their back or elderly with walking sticks are also a common sight. They will definitely serve as motivation for you to trek your way up to the peak!

A buddhist offering prayers facing Taktsang Monastery

Set on a rocky cliff high above Paro valley, Taktsang Monastery is one of the most impressive temples in the world

Tachog Lhakhang

Tachog Lhakhang, also known as Tashog or Tamchhog, is a small private temple located around 15 km into the journey from Paro to Thimphu. The temple was built in the 16th century by a renowned mahasiddha or practitioner of yoga and tantra, Thangtong Gyalpo. He is also known as the great 'Iron Bridge Builder' in the kingdom who built 58 iron suspension bridges, 111 stupas and many monasteries throughout the Himalayan region. To reach the temple, you will need to cross one of the eight suspension bridges he built in Bhutan. Crossing this ancient bridge is quite an adventure for some travellers.

Kyichu Lhakhang

The 7th century Kyichu Lhakhang, also known as Lho Kyerchu or Kyerchu, is the oldest and one of the most beautiful temples in Bhutan. Bhutanese revere the temple as a sacred jewel of Bhutan. The original temple was said to have been built overnight and used to be a smaller structure before the monastery was expanded. This spectacular temple has a tranquil and serene ambience that fosters a contemplative space. The elderly come to circumambulate the temple while chanting mantras and spinning prayer wheels. There is also a landscaped garden outside with an extraordinary orange tree in the courtyard that bears fruits all year round!

Cross the timeless old iron bridge of Bhutan

A majestic ancient temple from the 7th century

Jangtsa Dumtseg Lhakhang

Jangtsa Dumtseg Lhakhang is a unique temple located at Shari village in Paro valley. Unlike the other traditional Buddhist temples, the shape and design of this temple is modelled after a stupa. It is believed that Thangthong Gyalpo, the 'Iron Bridge Builder', constructed the temple around 1433. He subdued a powerful earth elemental spirit, and a subterranean serpentine spirit called a Lunyen. Both of them were malicious and caused much suffering and illness, such as leprosy, to the people residing in the area.

Tips

You have to be careful while visiting the temple as steep wooden ladders connect the floors and it is very dark inside.

The temple is a three-storey structure with each floor representing the three realms of heaven, earth, and hell, respectively.

A unique feature of the temple is the four sets of iron chains extending from the central tower and bound to the roof of the temple. According to local legends, the central tower, if left unchained, would fly off to Tibet.

You may need to rely on your mobile phone lights to navigate your way when you are inside

Dra Karpo

Dra Karpo, 'Split Rock', is a popular pilgrimage site in Paro valley. The location is believed to have been visited by Guru Rinpoche, who brought Buddhism to Bhutan, and his consort, Yeshey Tshogay. Since then, several Buddhist masters have visited Dra Karpo over the centuries.

Pilgrims circumambulate the mountainside 108 times over three to four days to gain merit and blessings. Of course, one can also do the short version of completing 13 rounds instead of 108; this will take about half an hour to 45 minutes.

The locals believe that circumambulating Dra Karpo will cleanse one's obscurations and bring about the highest level of spiritual attainment.

The site also attracted global attention when the international star Jet Li meditated there during his visit to Bhutan.

Kila Goenpa

Kila Goenpa is one of the oldest nunneries in Bhutan. In the 19th century, it was initially a meditation site. Fire destroyed the site, but it was restored much later by the 25th Chief Abbot of Bhutan, Sherub Gyeltshen. The Royal Government of Bhutan established the nunnery in 1968. Kila Goenpa is home to nuns who are engaged in Buddhist studies. One can see maroon-clad nuns entering and exiting the buildings that were built precariously on the face of a cliff.

To reach the nunnery, you have to hike for an hour from Chele La Pass. The hike is mostly downhill, cutting through dense coniferous forests. The nunnery has seven small temples and several meditation huts.

Dra Karpo is a very holy pilgrimage site

The nuns at Kila Goemba lead simple lives

Zuri Dzong

Zuri Dzong is located above Paro Rinpung Dzong and the National Museum known as Taa Dzong. It is one of the oldest dzongs in Bhutan, built in 1352. It was previously named 'Namthang Karpo' by Guru Rinpoche. Yung Toen Dorji, a disciple of Zuri Jampa Singye, later changed it to 'Zuri'.

In the early days, Zuri Dzong served as a watchtower along with Taa Dzong because of their strategic location and clear panoramic view of Paro valley.

Even though the dzong is smaller than most fortresses in Bhutan, the journey towards the dzong is highly rewarding. The hike is approximately 1.5 hours from the National Museum and an hour from COMO Uma Paro Resort.

You'll need to cross a small bridge to reach Zuri Dzong.

Zuri Dzong has one of the best viewpoints of Paro valley

Paro Dzong

Paro Dzong, also known as Rinpung Dzong, or the 'Fortress of the Heaps of Jewels', is a very distinguished building in the Paro district. You can catch a glimpse of it while your flight is landing at Paro International Airport. The dzong was built in 1644 under the instruction of Zhabdrung Ngawang Namgyal. Formerly, it served as a fort to defend Paro valley against invasions from Tibet. This ancient fortress is closely situated near Paro town and is easily accessible. During the popular Paro Tshechu, usually held in March, thousands of people flock to the courtyard of the dzong in their finest attire to join in the special occasion.

Some of the scenes from Bernardo Bertolucci's 1993 movie 'Little Buddha' were also filmed in Paro Dzong.

Paro Dzong is only a 15-minute walk from Paro Town

Drukgyel Dzong

The ancient ruins of Drukgyel Dzong is a famous archaeological site in Bhutan, located on a ridge in the upper Paro valley. It was constructed in 1649 and served as an important defence base in the region until 1951, when fire almost wrecked it completely.

Unlike the other ancient fortresses in the country, Drukgyel Dzong is the only dzong used for defensive purposes without any religious or administrative functions. The existing ruins and original defence structure of the dzong have been well-preserved through recent renovations.

The fort is located on top of a hill with steep cliffs on three sides and a single entrance to ensure that it is not vulnerable to attacks. It is heavily guarded by several watchtowers situated between the entrance and the foot of the hill.

There used to be tunnels providing protected passages for people to fetch water from the river at the foot of the hill, but these tunnels are now sealed.

Drugyel Dzong, a historic landmark that was crumbling with age, has now been restored

Dobji Dzong

Dobji Dzong is considered considered the first model dzong of Bhutan. Lama Ngawang Chogyal, the brother of the famous Drukpa Kuenley, built the dzong in 1531. The dzong is perched atop the large ridge overseeing the Thimphu-Phuentsholing Highway. Legend has it that Lama Ngawang Chogyal found a suitable site to build the dzong at the current place while looking for the spring source that originated below the throne of Jetsun Milarepa in Tibet.

Beneath the dzong, there is healing spring water trickling out of the rocky mountain. The locals believe that if one drinks or washes their heads and other body parts with deep devotion, the holy water will cure illnesses: headache, skin rashes, rheumatism, ulcer, gastritis, or stomach ache.

This 16th century dzong sits atop a ridge that now overlooks one of Bhutan's main highways

Namgay Artisanal Brewery

Namgay Artisanal Brewery is one of Bhutan's pioneer breweries in the craft beer industry. The brewery enjoys the distinction of being Bhutan's only brewpub and the second craft brewery operating in the country.

With a brewing capacity of 2000 litres, Namgay Artisanal Brewery has been churning out several craft beers that have become household favourites within a short span of time since its opening in 2016. Their flagship and best-selling beer is the Red Rice Lager, an easy-to-drink lager brewed with locally sourced red rice that adds subtle nutty notes and slight sweetness to the palate.

Inform your tour agency to book a brewery tour in advance should you wish to tour the brewery attached to the brewpub. The brewery is closed on Tuesdays in observance of dry day in Bhutan where liquor sale is prohibited.

They also brew dark ales, wheat beers, and apple ciders. These beers are available in any liquor outlet in Bhutan. However, if you wish to sample more beers that are not available in bottles, a visit to the brewpub is recommended. Apart from sampling the bottled and draft beers, Namgay Brewery offers other beers only available at the brewpub. Be sure to look out for their seasonal beers too.

Chill and unwind with some good local food and beers at Namgay Artisanal Brewery

You'll enjoy Aum Choden Homestay if you like immersing yourself in local culture

Aum Choden Homestay

Aum Choden Homestay is a two-storey traditional Bhutanese house that is 108 years old. It has a rustic charm that will leave you feeling rejuvenated.

An authentic Bhutanese experience you can have in the Land of Thunder Dragon is definitely pampering yourself with a hot stone bath!

Soaking in a medicinal hot stone bath is recommended for those who would like to immerse themselves in the local culture.

The locals usually take a hot stone bath once or twice weekly. They believe that these baths have healing properties. Medicinal hot stone baths are believed to be able to help alleviate some health issues such as stomach ache, hypertension, arthritis or joint pains.

At the homestay, visitors can take part in activities such as archery, darts, trying out the traditional dress, and watching demonstrations of Bhutanese cooking.

Chencho Weaving House

At Chencho Weaving House, also known as Traditional Weaving House, you'll see skilful women weavers apply their impeccable skills as they weave textiles out of cotton, silk, and other yarns.

You'll also get first-hand experience with the looms used to weave the textiles and understand the processes involved in producing handwoven textiles. A wide range of handwoven textiles is also available for you to browse through.

Chele La Pass

Chele La Pass is the highest mountain pass in Bhutan at 3,810 m, situated between Paro and Haa valley. The drive to the pass takes approximately two hours from Paro. The journey offers superb views and brings you through thick, dense forests. If you are lucky and the skies are clear, you'll see the magnificent Mount Jomolhari, Jichu Drake and other spectacular peaks from the pass. You'll be mesmerised by the stunning mountain views, fluttering prayer flags and lush green valleys from this vantage point.

You can find a vast collection of Bhutanese textiles at Chencho Weaving House

Chele La Pass offers a superb view of the Himalayan range

Haa

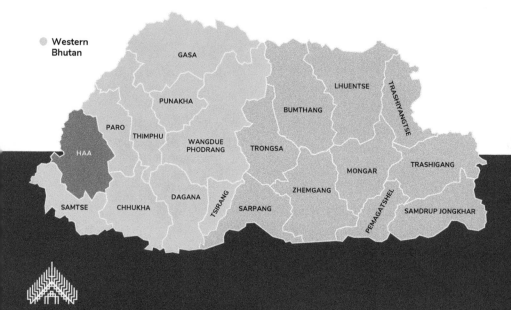

Western Bhutan

GASA

LHUENTSE

TRASHIYANGTSE

PUNAKHA

BUMTHANG

PARO

THIMPHU

WANGDUE PHODRANG

TRONGSA

HAA

MONGAR

TRASHIGANG

ZHEMGANG

DAGANA

TSIRANG

PEMAGATSHEL

SAMTSE

CHHUKHA

SARPANG

SAMDRUP JONGKHAR

Haa is one of the most beautiful and pristine places in Bhutan, with untouched natural beauty. Another name of Haa is 'Hidden Land of Rice Valley'. It is one of the smallest districts and least populated valleys in Bhutan.

The Haa district borders Tibet, and is the ancestral home of the Royal Grandmother. If you are looking for a peaceful getaway, Haa district is a great option to unwind and embrace tranquillity.

Haa valley is also a paradise for hikers and trekkers as some of the best trekking and mountain biking routes are found around this area. The most popular festival for the Haa community is the Haa Summer Festival usually held in July.

Attractions

- Lhakhang Karpo
- Lhakhang Nagpo
- Shelkar Drak
- Chhundu Lhakhang
- Haa Dzong
- Juneydrak Hermitage

Lhakhang Karpo

Lhakhang Nagpo

Lhakhang Karpo and Lhakhang Nagpo are two of the 108 monasteries built by Tibetan King Songtsen Gampo in the 7th century. It is believed that the King had released two pigeons, a white and black one, to allocate the sites for the two temples. The area where the white pigeon landed was chosen for construction and named Lhakhang Karpo, 'white temple'. Lhakhang Karpo is situated at the foothills of three towering mountains known as Rigsum Gonpo, 'Lord of Three Families'.

Lhakhang Karpo houses the monastic body for the Haa region, and festivals are usually held in this temple. The architecture of the temple reflects its name as it is mainly white in colour with Bhutanese design. There is also a colossal door intricately carved to welcome visitors to the temple. Buddhist paintings and murals decorate the interior temple walls.

Lhakhang Nagpo, 'black temple', one of the oldest temples in Haa valley, is just a 15-minute walk behind Lhakhang Karpo. It is said that the black pigeon landed at the site when King Songtsen released it. Thus, the temple was named Lhakhang Nagpo. The temple was incredibly built on a lake, and one can access it through an opening on the temple's floor.

In contrast to Lhakhang Karpo, the temple is elegantly painted in black. And unlike Lhakhang Karpo, there aren't any monk quarters on this site. The only resident you'll find within the temple area is the caretaker who lives in a small hut.

Most festivals in Haa are held in Lhakhang Karpo

Legend says that a mermaid spirit resides on the lake

Shelkar Drak

A short hike up the valley behind Lhakhang Karpo is Shelkar Drak, 'Crystal Cliff'. Shelkar Drak is a small retreat centre perched on a limestone cliff. To get to Shelkar Drak, you have to drive from Dumcho bridge towards Takchu Goenpa. At the turn below Lungtsho village, walk for half an hour to reach the temple. Above Shelkar Drak, there is a flatland where it is said that the fortunate can see a lake and a variety of fruits.

Chhundu Lhakhang

Chhundu Lhakhang is one of the temples dedicated to honour the valley's protective deity, Ap Chhundu. A visit to the temple will help you understand the interesting history of the valley. Legend has it that Ap Chhundu was banished to Haa by Zhabdrung after an altercation with Gyenyen, Thimphu's protector. He is also said to have quarrelled with Paro's guardian, Jichu Drakye.

The views from Shelkar Drak are absolutely breathtaking

Legend has it that Haa Dzong was built to hold back the evil influences of the serpent deities

Juneydrak Hermitage

Juneydrak Hermitage, also known as Juneydrag, is a small temple dedicated to Guru Rinpoche. The temple is situated at 2,930 m above sea level. The hike to Juneydrak Hermitage takes about 45 minutes from Katsho Village. Locals believe that Guru Rinpoche visited this place and subdued a demon. It's also believed that Guru Rinpoche placed the eye and fang of the demon on the cliff. This cliffside retreat also houses the right footprint of Machig Labdrön, a female Tibetan tantric practitioner whose practice of Chöd has heavily influenced all schools of Tibetan Buddhism.

Haa Dzong

Haa Dzong was established in 1895 after the appointment of the first head of the sub-district. The dzong was meant to protect the adjoining border from Tibetan invasions. A new dzong was constructed after the fire destroyed the dzong in 1913. In 1963, the dzong was handed over to the Indian army to be used as an army training camp. And in 1968, a new dzong was again constructed and continues to function as the district administrative headquarters.

At Juneydrak Hermitage, you see different naturally formed sacred shapes on the rocks

Samtse, Chhukha and Dagana districts are currently still under development for tourism.

● Western Bhutan

GASA

PUNAKHA

LHUENTSE

TRASHIYANGTSE

BUMTHANG

PARO

THIMPHU

WANGDUE PHODRANG

TRONGSA

HAA

MONGAR

TRASHIGANG

DAGANA

TSIRANG

ZHEMGANG

SAMTSE

CHHUKHA

SARPANG

PEMAGATSHEL

SAMDRUP JONGKHAR

Dagana

Dagana is a small district in the southwest of Bhutan, a place for nature lovers due to its picturesque environment. Over 80% of the district is under forest cover, giving it a rugged and impressive landscape. Located below the major valleys of Thimphu and Wangdue Phodrang, Dagana stretches down to Bhutan's southern border. It's also a paradise for bird watchers as it is home to various bird species. An iconic highlight of Dagana is the three sacred stone megaliths: Do Namkhai Kaw 'Sky Pillar Rock', Do Kelpai Genthey 'The Rock of Ancient Steps' and Tha Namkhai Dzong 'The Frontier Sky Fortress'.

Chhukha

Chhukha is located in the dense subtropical forests region of southwestern Bhutan. Phuentsholing, the main trade city in Chhukha and a border town to the Indian town of Jaigaon, is a dynamic place.

There are two major ethnic groups in Chhukha, the Ngalops and the Lhothampas, making the district culturally diverse. Aside from celebrating Buddhist festivals, there are also other festivals and practices embraced in Chhukha. An important feature of the district is the two hydropower projects: Chhukha and Tala Hydropower Projects. Tala, the biggest joint project between Bhutan and India, serves as the largest revenue of Bhutan.

Samtse

Samtse is a tranquil subtropical district that is away from all the hustle and bustle of the city. The district is located in the most southwestern region of Bhutan. The main source of income for these communities come from agriculture and the construction industry. The district is home to a diverse range of flora and fauna. You can also find exotic animals like local elephants in Samtse. An important part of the district is the Samtse College of Education, established in 1968 and deemed one of Bhutan's leading educational institutions.

Shivalaya Mandir

The mandir (Hindu temple) in Samtse was rebuilt upon the command of the fifth King. To commemorate the royal wedding in 2011, the King gifted the temple to the people of Samtse. The temple was constructed with intricately carved sandstone and features marble statues of Lord Shiva and other Hindu deities. It was built around a sacred site where a small temple was previously located. The mandir's construction was completed in 2015, coinciding with the 60th birthday of the fourth King, Jigme Singye Wangchuck, and consecrated on February 6, 2016, on the birth of His Royal Highness Crown Prince Jigme Namgyel Wangchuck. The 15 m high temple is an iconic site of the Samtse district.

Shivalaya Mandir is the first Hindu temple in Bhutan that is devoted to Lord Shiva

Tsirang

Western Bhutan

GASA

PUNAKHA

PARO

THIMPHU

HAA

WANGDUE PHODRANG

LHUENTSE

TRASHIYANGTSE

BUMTHANG

TRONGSA

MONGAR

TRASHIGANG

DAGANA

TSIRANG

ZHEMGANG

SAMTSE

CHHUKHA

SARPANG

PEMAGATSHEL

SAMDRUP JONGKHAR

Tsirang district is located in the southwestern part of Bhutan along the Wangdue-Gelephu Highway. One of the country's longest rivers, Punatsang Chhu, also known as Sankosh River, flows through the Tsirang district. Nepali language and Dzongkha are spoken in the district as it is the central district where majority of the Lhotshampa population reside. In Tsirang, you can see colourful flowers brightening the traditional Lhotshampa houses.

Attractions

- Pemachoeling Heritage Forest
- Rigsum Pemai Dumra
- Hindu-Buddhist Temple
- Namgyel Chholing Rabdey Dratsang
- Birdwatching Point

Pemachoeling Heritage Forest

The Pemachoeling Heritage Forest was inaugurated in 2017 as an ecotourism site in Tsirang. The heritage forest is located around 30 km away from Damphu town. It is a sacred sanctuary rich with wildlife, such as the endangered royal Bengal tigers. The historical site serves to protect the natural forests and preserve the spiritual values attached to the site. There is a footpath from the ruins of an ancient fortress to a sacred pilgrimage site. The uphill hike takes about 30 minutes. The locals believe that a powerful king called Sang Sup Gyap ruled the ancient fortress around 200 years ago.

Hindu-Buddhist Temple

An interesting site in the Tsirang district is a Hindu-Buddhist temple situated right in the heart of Damphu town. It showcases the Hindu and Buddhist cultures that coexist harmoniously in the country.

The temple was built with two different entrances, with the Buddhist temple to the right and the Hindu temple on the left. Here, you will find one of the largest statues of Guru Rinpoche near the temple.

A Buddhist and Hindu temple uniquely housed next to each other under the same roof

Rigsum Pemai Dumra

Rigsum Pemai Dumra is a beautiful recreational park that is popular with tourists and locals alike. There are two huge gazebos, mesmerising fountains, a prayer wheel and an artificial lake for all the park-goers to enjoy. The park is a refreshing getaway from the hustle-bustle of city life. The park usually comes alive during the weekend with families and friends having picnics and get-togethers.

Namgyel Chholing Rabdey Dratsang

Tsirang Namgyel Chholing Rabdey Dratsang is the venue for Buddhist rituals and the annual Tsirang Tshechu. The annual festival is the biggest festival in the southern town of Tsirang. The masked dance festival, usually held in March, attracts people from all over the region.

Namgyel Chholing Rabdey Dratsang was designed in traditional Bhutanese architecture style

A beautiful mangrove blue flycatcher

Birdwatching Point

For those who enjoy birdwatching, Tsirang will be a paradise. The birdwatching point is located just above the national highway near Sankosh bridge. It's home to some rare birds like the rufous-necked hornbill, great hornbill, oriental turtle, grey treepie, paddy-field pipit, blue whistling thrush, jungle babbler, and black eagle. Even if you are not into birdwatching, do keep a lookout for these beautiful flying creatures. Aside from birds, you can also see a variety of butterfly species in the area.

Wangdue Phodrang

Western
Bhutan

GASA

PUNAKHA

LHUENTSE

TRASHIYANGTSE

BUMTHANG

PARO

THIMPHU

WANGDUE
PHODRANG

TRONGSA

HAA

MONGAR

TRASHIGANG

ZHEMGANG

DAGANA

TSIRANG

SAMTSE

CHHUKHA

SARPANG

PEMAGATSHEL

SAMDRUP JONGKHAR

Wangdue Phodrang, also commonly known as Wangdue, is the last town on the west side of the highway before entering central Bhutan. It is the second-largest district in Bhutan and has extremely varied climatic conditions, ranging from the subtropical climate in the south to cool and snowy regions in the north.

Most of the district is environmentally protected. Wangdue Phodrang district is home to many rare and exotic animals like red pandas, royal Bengal tigers and snow leopards. There are also many rare birds such as the black-necked cranes, white-bellied herons and the spotted eagles. On top of that, the district is famous for its fine bamboo work and slate carvings.

Attractions

- Gangtey/Phobjikha Valley
- Gangtey Goemba
- Black-necked Crane Festival
- Thenkhor Yuetshe Trek
- Rada Lhakhang
- Gaselo and Nahee Village
- Rinchengang Village

Gangtey / Phobjikha Valley

Gangtey, also popularly known as Phobjikha Valley, is an impressive site in Wangdue Phodrang district. The picturesque valley is set against the backdrop of the Black Mountain range. It is a U-shaped valley with breathtaking views and abundant yaks that arrive from higher altitudes to seek warmth from the freezing weather. The lush green valley with its notable marshland is popular for its awe-inspiring sceneries. Phobjikha Valley is easily a tourist's favourite and a must-visit place in Bhutan.

Tips

Winter is the best time to be in Gangtey because of the crisp blue skies and chilly weather. If you visit during the winter season, you have an opportunity to watch the majestic black-necked cranes fly through the valleys. Do ensure that you bring along some thick winter clothes to keep warm. Aside from winter, Gangtey is also an ideal place to visit during spring due to the perfect weather conditions and beautiful blooms in the valley.

If you're a nature lover, Gangtey is a must-have on your itinerary

Tenkhor Yuetshe Trek (Gangtey Nature Trail)

Tenkhor Yuetshe trek is ideal for those who wish to take a leisure walk while traversing through a cluster of charming villages. It's a relatively easy 4 km hike that takes around 1.5 to four hours to complete. It's also one of the shortest nature trails in Bhutan. Your journey begins at the Gangtey Monastery and will take you downhill through the pine forest to a traditional village known as Semchubara. You'll continue to hike upwards, following a dirt road that will lead you to Jangchub Kemba village. The path will continue through the primary marshland of the valley and ends in Khewa Lhakhang. You will pass through some spectacular portions of the valley.

Black-necked Crane Festival

The Black-necked Crane Festival is celebrated annually on 11 November, coinciding with the birthday of the fourth King, Jigme Singye Wangchuck. The festival showcases Bhutanese cultural heritage through masked folk dances and songs, raising awareness about conservation issues. It is a special occasion held at the courtyard of Gangtey Goemba where locals celebrate the arrival of the endangered and majestic birds from the Tibetan Plateau. The black-necked cranes are amongst the rarest cranes in the world and they migrate to Phobjikha Valley during the winter months between October and February. There is a Black-necked Crane Information Centre in Phobjikha Valley where you can learn more about the protection and conservation efforts of these graceful birds.

The locals revere the black-necked cranes as a symbol of longevity, peace, and prosperity

Gangtey Goemba

Gangtey Goemba or Gangtey Monastery is a beautiful temple located on the hilltop, overlooking the stunning Phobjikha Valley. The temple was founded in 1613 by Gyalse Pema Thinley, the grandson and the reincarnation of the great treasure revealer, Pema Lingpa. It is not just the locals who visit this humble and simple temple; the black-necked cranes circle the temple clockwise three times, when they arrive and before they depart from their winter home. How sacred and mystical!

The main hall in the monastery, known as the tshokhang, was built in Tibetan architectural style

Gaselo and Nahee Village

The two villages are located towards the western side of Wangdue Phodrang district. It takes about two hours to reach Gaselo and Nahee village. These traditional villages are ideal spots for you to picnic during the daytime and experience an authentic Bhutanese rural lifestyle. You'll get to enjoy the simplicity of farming life in Bhutan. If you visit during early summer, you'll be captivated by the traditional methods used by the farmers during rice plantation. Autumn is also a good time to visit the villages to experience the harvest festival. You'll get to share in the happiness of the farmers over their bountiful harvest.

Rada Lhakhang

Rada Lhakhang, also known as the Temple of Sha Radap, is situated close to Wangdue Phodrang Dzong. It is dedicated to the worship of the local guardian deity known as Sha Radap. Locals often pay a visit to this temple to seek blessings and also for naming ceremonies. The names given to the newborns usually start with 'Rada'.

If you have a specific wish in mind, you can also visit the temple to roll some dice to see if your prayer will be answered. If the outcome of your dice is the auspicious number of 7, 11 or 13, it indicates that your wishes will be fulfilled.

Rada Lhakhang is a popular worship site for the local community

Rinchengang Village

Rinchengang is a small clustered village located opposite Wangdue Phodrang Dzong. The village is famous for its stonemasonry skills. It takes about 20 minutes to walk uphill to reach the village. From here, there is a great view of the dzong, valley and river. It is definitely worth a visit for those looking for a rustic village experience.

Proverb

བཟོཕ་མང་ན་སྒོ་ལྡིང་མི་ཚུགས།

Zow mangna go lhong mi tshu.

When there are too many carpenters, the door cannot be erected.

To get a glimpse of an authentic rural lifestyle, pay a visit to Rinchegang village

Gasa

Western Bhutan

GASA
PUNAKHA
LHUENTSE
TRASHIYANGTSE
BUMTHANG
PARO
THIMPHU
WANGDUE PHODRANG
TRONGSA
HAA
MONGAR
TRASHIGANG
ZHEMGANG
DAGANA
TSIRANG
SARPANG
PEMAGATSHEL
SAMTSE
CHHUKHA
SAMDRUP JONGKHAR

Gasa is the northernmost district of Bhutan. This enchanting region has exceptionally long and cold winters and short pleasant summers. It has the smallest population in the country, with merely 3,000 inhabitants. The main source of revenue in Gasa is from trading products made from yaks. When you visit the district, you can find yak hair textiles, cheese, butter and yak meat. The community also harvest and sell cordyceps, a highly valued medicinal fungus.

In addition, the district is also well-known for its indigenous communities, the Layaps, from Laya village. Gasa is an incredible place to savour the natural beauty and tranquillity of the kingdom.

To experience Gasa, consider taking up some of the most scenic treks in Bhutan, such as Jomolhari Trek, Laya-Gasa Trek, Merak-Sakteng Trek or the world's toughest trek, Snowman Trek.

Attractions

- Gasa Dzong
- Gasa Tshachu
- Laya Village
- Lunana Village

Gasa Dzong

Gasa Dzong, locally known as Tashi Thongmon Dzong, was built by Zhabdrung in 1646 to commemorate the victories over the Tibetans. It later defended the country against several invasions in the 17th and 18th century. Unlike the other dzongs in the country, this ancient fortress is uniquely circular, with three watchtowers placed strategically to overlook the valley.

Gasa Tshachu

The hot spring located close to the banks of Mo Chhu River in Gasa is one of the most popular springs in Bhutan. Both locals and tourists often visit Gasa Tsachu to soak in the medicinal properties of the spring water. It is a frequently visited site in this least populated district of Bhutan, especially during the winter season. There are five bathhouses at Gasa Tshachu for the general public and one reserved for the royals.

On clear days, expect a spectacular view of the mountains from Gasa Dzong

Laya Village

Laya village is one of the smallest settlements in the kingdom, located at an elevation of 3,800 m. As of now, the only way to explore the village is via a two-day trek starting from Gasa town. The 28 km hike is not very difficult but you'll have to trek through muddy and slippery terrains to reach this mesmerising village. However, the good news is that a road is currently being constructed from Gasa to Laya. One day, you might no longer need to hike your way to Laya anymore.

Laya village has around 110 houses and is home to the Layap community. The Layaps have their distinct dialect and traditional dress that are different from mainstream Bhutanese society. The Layap women are easily identifiable with their yak wool garments and conical hats.

If you are a history buff, you'll definitely enjoy mingling with the semi-nomadic tribes to learn about their unique culture.

You'll also come across Bhutan's national animal, takin, or the exotic national flower, blue poppy in the village.

Lunana Village

Lunana is a hidden gem of Bhutan and the most remote settlement in the country. In the village, you can experience the culture of nomads living amongst the glaciers. The Lunaps make their living from yaks and sheep. The nomads are also very well-versed in medicinal herbs and earn extra income from cordyceps harvesting.

A charming feature of Lunana village is its unspoiled environment. During winters, Lunana experiences heavy snowfall and the mountain passes become inaccessible to the neighbouring districts. The snowfall causes the Lunap community to be isolated from the outside world for six months a year.

Healthcare and education is a challenge for the Lunaps due to the remoteness of the region. The government provides grants to encourage teachers to work in remote areas to help educate the children.

You can experience the beauty of this untouched gem by attempting one of the world's most demanding hikes, the Snowman Trek. Alternatively, you can also opt for a luxury Himalayan experience and take a helicopter ride to Lunana.

The two-day Royal Highland Festival, an annual celebration of nomadic highlander traditions in Laya, is a popular festival for the highlanders. On every 24 & 25 October, highlanders of all ethnicities congregate in Laya to showcase their cultures.

Check out Royal Highland Festival

s.bn.sg/highlandfest

Village life often revolves around yak herding, an important means of survival for the highlanders

A horse racing competition is held at Royal Highland Festival to showcase the yak herders' dexterity

Bumthang

Central Bhutan

GASA

PUNAKHA

LHUENTSE

TRASHIYANGTSE

PARO

THIMPHU

WANGDUE PHODRANG

BUMTHANG

HAA

TRONGSA

MONGAR

TRASHIGANG

DAGANA

TSIRANG

ZHEMGANG

PEMAGATSHEL

SAMTSE

CHHUKHA

SARPANG

SAMDRUP JONGKHAR

Bumthang, literally translated as 'beautiful field', is a historic district in Bhutan where some of the oldest and most revered Buddhist temples are found, including the 7th century Jambay Lhakhang. Bumthang, also known as Jakar, is located in central Bhutan. It was here that Buddhism was first introduced to Bhutan. The district comprises four valleys: Choekhor, Tang, Chumey and Ura. Bumthang is also famous for the production of wheat, buckwheat, dairy products and potatoes. Beautiful apple orchards and dairy farms are common sights in this district.

Bumthang is also home to Bathpalathang Airport, one of the three domestic airports in Bhutan.

Attractions

- Kurjey Lhakhang
- Jambay Lhakhang
- Jakar Dzong
- Mebar Tsho (Burning Lake)
- Bumthang Brewery and Cheese Factory
- Yathra Weaving Centre

Kurjey Lhakhang

Nestled on the side of a hill and surrounded by 108 chorten walls, the complex houses three revered temples. This large temple complex is filled with great religious significance. The main attraction of Kurjey Lhakhang is the upper floor of the oldest temple, built in the 17th century. You can find 1000 small statues of Guru Rinpoche at the temple. Locals believe that a path behind the wall on the upper floor leads to a meditative cave prohibited for public access. The cave is where Guru Rinpoche left his body imprint on the rock and meditated for three months in the 8th century. There is also a huge cypress tree near the temple entrance, which is believed to have sprouted from Guru Rinpoche's walking stick.

It is said that you can clear your bad karma by crawling through a narrow rock passage at Kurjey Lhakhang

Jambay Lhakhang

According to legend, this temple was one of the 108 temples built by the Tibetan King Songtsen Gampo in the 7th century within a single day. The tale states that the Tibetan King built a series of temples throughout the Himalayas to pin down the different parts of an ogress. Four were built to pin down her shoulders and hips, four more for the elbows and knees, and four to hold down her hands and feet. It was believed that Jambay Lhakhang was built to pin down the left knee of the ogress.

The single-storey complex is famous for its annual festival Jambay Lhakhang Drup as much as for its legends. The festival's main highlight is a sacred dance, known as Ter Cham, where masked dancers perform naked at midnight. In the evening, there is Mewang, a fire blessing ceremony where the devotees jump over flames to wash away their bad karma.

Jakar Dzong

Jakar Dzong or Jakar Yugyal Dzong is the dzong of the Bumthang district. It is located on a ridge above Jakar town in the Chamkhar (Choekhor) valley. Jakar means 'white bird', and Jakar Dzong is known as the 'Fortress of White Bird'. It is said that a white bird flew and perched on the ridge where Jakar Dzong is situated.

There are two unique features of the fortress that sets it apart from other fortresses in the country. Firstly, the utse (central tower) is 50 m high and secondly, the fortress has two parallel walls interconnected by fortified towers, which provide the population access to water in the case of a siege.

Traditionally, the dzong played an important role as the fortress of defence of the eastern districts. It was also the seat of the first King of Bhutan.

Jambay Lhakhang is an ancient Buddhist site

Jakar Dzong overlooks the beautiful Chokhor valley

Bumthang Brewery and Cheese Factory

The wide and open valley of Bumthang is the production centre for Bhutan's Swiss cheese and various local brews. A Swiss national, Fritz Maurer founded a micro-brewery and Swiss farm in Bumthang in 1996. Fritz married a Bhutanese and set up the first-of-its-kind brewery in Bhutan, producing draught beer, apple cider, wine, apple brandy and juice. This brewery also produces the famous Bhutanese 'Red Panda Beer', an unfiltered, preservative-free brew. The beers are prepared in an old-school manner.

There is also a Swiss farm that produces a variety of Swiss cheese and is the first commercial cheese factory in Bhutan. Check out the large round cheese on the drying shelves. They are often fully booked even before they're ready for eating.

Fritz Maurer is also credited for introducing modern farming equipment, green technology that is fuel-efficient, and smokeless wood stoves that are widely used in Bumthang and Bhutan today.

The brewery and cheese factory are located next to each other, so feel free to pop over for a taste of Bhutanese beer and cheese when you are in Bumthang.

Gigantic cheese made in Bhutan

Yathra Weaving Centre

Yathra is colourful wool, weaved with intricate patterns native to Chumey valley in Bumthang. Traditionally, every household in Chumey owns a backstrap loom and girls are taught how to weave from a very young age. Yaks and sheep wool is used for weaving because the thick fabric is ideal for the cold weather in Bumthang.

You can see women skilfully weaving intricate designs on their backstrap loom and dying wools using natural dyes. The women in Chumey weave throughout the year as it is their main source of income. Thus, yathra products such as jackets, throws and bags are souvenirs uniquely from Bumthang.

Mebar Tsho (Burning Lake)

This beautiful freshwater lake is a popular attraction in Bumthang. Colourful prayer flags surround the picturesque and legendary lake. It is said that the famous treasure revealer, Pema Lingpa jumped into the lake and re-emerged with treasures in his hand: a chest, a scroll of paper and a butter lamp that was still burning bright! Thus, the sacred site is known as Burning Lake.

You can also find stacks of tsa-tsas or small offerings around the lake area. Tsa-tsas are sacred objects moulded from clay mixed with the ashes of the deceased. You can find these miniature stupas in caves, underneath rocks, alongside the roads or any place sheltered from the elements.

Bereaved families commission these tsatsa offerings in honour of their loved ones

The calmness and serenity of Mebar Tsho will take all your worries away

Trongsa

Central
Bhutan

GASA

PUNAKHA

LHUENTSE

TRASHIYANGTSE

BUMTHANG

PARO

THIMPHU

WANGDUE
PHODRANG

TRONGSA

HAA

MONGAR

TRASHIGANG

DAGANA

ZHEMGANG

TSIRANG

PEMAGATSHEL

SAMTSE

CHHUKHA

SARPANG

SAMDRUP JONGKHAR

Trongsa, formerly known as Tongsa, is the capital of Trongsa district, located in central Bhutan. Trongsa district was once an important district as it was the headquarters for the eastern region and the seat of the Trongsa governor.

Tradition also dictates that the king of Bhutan has to take on the role of Trongsa Penlop (governor) before becoming the crown prince and eventually the king.

Attractions

- Trongsa Dzong
- Chendebji Chorten
- Kuenga Rabten Palace
- Royal Heritage Museum (Tower of Trongsa)
- Sangchen Ogyen Tsuklag Monastery

Trongsa Dzong

The magnificent Trongsa Dzong is easily noticeable from anywhere in town. This ancient fortress was built in 1644 and used to be the seat of the Wangchuck dynasty before they became the rulers of Bhutan in 1907. This massive dzong is the largest fortress in Bhutan, located on a spur overlooking the gorge of the Mangdi Chuu river. The size, strategic location and grand architecture of the dzong renders it one of the most impressive dzongs in the country.

The first two Bhutanese Kings ruled the country from this ancient fortress

Kuenga Rabten Palace

An hour to the south of Trongsa lies the winter palace of the second King of Bhutan, Jigme Wangchuck, which is now the National Commission for Cultural Affairs. En route to the palace, it's a beautiful drive passing through Takse Goemba, several huge waterfalls, quaint villages and rice terraces at the lower Mangde Chhu valley. Stone walls surround the Kuenga Rabten Palace with courtyards on three sides. The tall main building is located on the fourth side with two protruding aisles.

The ground and first floors used to be a storehouse and a military garrison. However, the ground floor is now empty, and the first floor is used as classrooms for the monks. On the second floor, there are three adjacent rooms. The main entrance leads into the central room, known as the Sangye Lhakhang, the main temple.

Next to the central room was the private residence of King Jigme Wangchuck and Queen Phuntsho Choden. The King's room is still very well-preserved to this day. During King Jigme Wangchuck's time in the palace, other rooms on the floor were used as guestrooms and to grant audiences.

Chendebji Chorten

Like the stupa in Sangchhen Dorji Lhuendrup Nunnery, the stupa in Chendebji Chorten was also constructed in Nepali style. It mimics the style of the Boudhanath Stupa in Kathmandu. The stupa was built in the 18th century by Buddhist Lama Ngesup Tshering Wangchuk to ward off evils.

There are several legends associated with the chorten. The most popular one is that the Chendebji Chorten was constructed on top of an evil spirit manifested in the form of a gigantic snake.

A long prayer wall adorned with Buddhist scriptures is also located in the compound.

Chendebji Chorten attracts many pilgrims during Lhundrup Molam Chenmo, a festival held annually in the ninth month of the Bhutanese calendar.

Proverb

མི་གཅིག་དགའ་བའི་བསོད་ནམས་ར་གིས་ཡང་འབག་མི་འཐེག།

Mi chi gawi soenam taa giya ba methey.

To give happiness to another person gives such great merit, it cannot even be carried by a horse.

Chendebji Chorten is also a popular picnic spot where you can simply sit down, eat and enjoy nature

Royal Heritage Museum

Officially called the Royal Heritage Museum, and locally known as Tower of Trongsa or Taa Dzong, this 17th century cylindrical five-storey tower is one of the top attractions in Trongsa. The first Trongsa Governor, Chogyal Minjur Tempa, built the museum in 1652. He strategically built the watchtower above Trongsa Dzong to guard the fortress from any attacks.

If you are a history buff who is keen to learn about the history of Buddhism in Bhutan or the history of the royal family, you should not miss this site. At the museum, you'll watch a 15-minute introduction video and get to explore 11 galleries. There are many interesting and sacred artefacts excellently exhibited on the five floors. The Royal Heritage Museum is a fascinating site with stunning views from the top of the tower. However, visitors are not allowed to bring in their camera or cell phones.

This is your opportunity to get up close to the Raven crown worn by the second King, Jigme Wangchuck

Sangchen Ogyen Tsuklag Monastery

Sangchen Ogyen Tsuklag Monastery, also known as Rephel Midrol Lhakhang is located in Samcholing village. It is approximately one hour drive from Trongsa town.

The main temple is a 1200-year-old two-storey building founded in the 8th century by the great female practitioner Khandro Tashi Khidren of Chhagkhar, a consort of Guru Rinpoche. The monastery is the custodian of some of Bhutan's most highly regarded religious treasures, such as a mandala mural depicting the deity Zhitro Lhatsog from the 8th century, a Buddha statue that is said to have spoken, and a treasure bell of Terton Sherab Mebar.

In late 2009, the people of Samcholing and Rephel community called for Khedrupchen Rinpoche to take over the monastery. They requested the Royal Government of Bhutan to offer the monastery to Khedrupchen Rinpoche — the fifth reincarnation of Khedrup Jigme Kundrol — who is a scholar and practitioner from the Longchen Nyingthik lineage. Khedrupchen Rinpoche accepted the request and renamed the monastery to Sangchen Ogyen Tsuklag. Since then, the monastery has been Rinpoche's main seat.

Khedrupchen Rinpoche is also the founder and president of Khedrup Foundation, a registered non-profit organisation in Bhutan. Under Rinpoche's guidance and patronage, the foundation manages a list of monasteries, initiatives and projects. Among other things, the foundation is mandated to promote equity and provide access to the learning and practice of the Buddha Dharma for monks and laymen alike. You can read the detailed interesting account of Rinpoche's lineage and previous incarnations at www.khedrupfoundation.org.

Khedrupchen Rinpoche's birth was accompanied by many miraculous signs

The centuries-old monastery is home to 45 monks

Khedrupchen Rinpoche travels around the world to teach Buddhism to his students at their request

Sarpang and Zhemgang districts are currently still under development for tourism.

● Central Bhutan

GASA

PUNAKHA

PARO

THIMPHU

HAA

WANGDUE PHODRANG

DAGANA

SAMTSE

CHHUKHA

TSIRANG

SARPANG

TRONGSA

LHUENTSE

TRASHIYANGTSE

BUMTHANG

ZHEMGANG

MONGAR

PEMAGATSHEL

TRASHIGANG

SAMDRUP JONGKHAR

Sarpang

Sarpang district is located in the central part of southern Bhutan and borders the state of Assam in India. Gelephu is a major town within the district and is one of the three gateways to Bhutan from India. There is also a domestic airport, Gelephu Airport, located in Gelephu town.

Sarpang is strategically located and has previously functioned as the headquarters for the administration of southern Bhutan. The district is culturally diverse, with Nepali being the dominant language spoken by the Lhotshampa community.

Zhemgang

Zhemgang is a district that is incredibly rich in biodiversity, with lush forests that are home to 22 endangered animal species. Royal Manas National Park also covers part of Zhemgang district. The district is known for being one of the last regions in Bhutan to follow ancient Bon (animism) traditions. Bonpo (Bon priests) are respected religious leaders in the region. The locals are also famous for their bamboo crafting and pottery skills. The local language of Zhemgang is known as Khengpa.

While Bhutan is one of the smallest countries in the world, its conservation efforts are one of the biggest

མདའ་རྒྱབ་ལོ་མི་གཙོ་གཏད་ལོ་གཙོ་བྱོ་སླབ་ལོ་མི་གཙོ་ཉན་ལོ་གཙོ།

Da chab lu mi tso, thi lu tso, lo lab lu mi tso, nyen lu tso.

The way the arrow hits the target is more important than the way it is shot;
the way you listen is more essential than the way you talk.

Samdrup Jongkhar

Eastern Bhutan

Samdrup Jongkhar town is located in the south-eastern part of Bhutan and borders the Indian state of Assam. It lies at an elevation of approximately 190 m and is known to be the oldest town in Bhutan and the largest urban centre in eastern Bhutan.

As a border town, merchants and tourists often use Samdrup Jongkhar to enter eastern Bhutan via land, especially if they intend to explore the districts in eastern Bhutan such as Trashigang, Trashiyangtse, Mongar and Lhuentse.

The road from Samdrup Jongkhar to Trashigang was completed in the 1960s, connecting the eastern and southern regions of the country. Given the road connection, the eastern region benefits from trade, primarily through trade across the Indian border.

Attractions

- Samdrup Jongkhar Dzong
- Rabdey Dratshang
- Zangdopelri Lhakhang
- Dewathang
- Mithun Breeding Farm

The easiest way to visit Samdrup Jongkhar would be to take a flight to Guwahati, India. You will need to apply for an Indian visa should you wish to travel to Samdrup Jongkhar by land. The drive from the airport to Samdrup Jongkhar will take approximately two to three hours. You will see the Assam tea plantations along the way.

Samdrup Jongkhar district in Bhutan is just steps away from Assam state in India

Samdrup Jongkhar Dzong

Samdrup Jongkhar Dzong is one of the newest dzongs in the country and serves as the office for district administrators. Unlike other dzongs in Bhutan, Samdrup Jongkhar Dzong was built on a flat and fairly wide-open area. The dzong was constructed in cement, a stark contrast to the older dzongs that were built in mud and clay bricks, with stones as the foundation.

Rabdey Dratshang

Next to Samdrup Jongkhar Dzong is the district monastic body, called Rabdey Dratshang, constructed in 2004. Rabdey Dratshang is the house for the monk body, and it has a number of new novices who are looked after by the religious representatives.

Mithun Breeding Farm

Mithun Breeding Farm is located at Orong, along the highway en route to Samdrup Jongkhar, above Dewathang town.

Mithuns are considered the finest breed of bison in Bhutan. These impressive cattle are well sought-after by cattle owners in Bhutan due to their easy maintenance and burly characteristics. Cattle breeders admire the mithuns for their ability to crossbreed with Siri breeds to produce superior-quality cattle breeds, jatsa and jatsum. These draught cattle are known for their high milk production.

Mithun Breeding Farm is the only farm in eastern Bhutan that breeds, raises and supplies mithuns to farmers in the six eastern districts of Bhutan. The farm is a popular tourist attraction as it provides excellent insights into the breeding process of mithuns.

Dewathang

Dewathang or Deothang is a gewog (village) settlement in Samdrup Jongkhar. Dewathang, 'Flat Area of Happiness', is a place with great historical significance, given its association with the Anglo-British war. Jigme Namgyal — father of Ugyen Wangchuck, the first King of Bhutan — led the battle against the British at this very site.

There is a bazaar in the village, and the army barracks of the Royal Bhutan Army controls the village entrance. Beyond the town, there is a technical college, a large hospital and a secondary school. Overlooking the village atop the hill is a Nyingma Buddhist tradition college, Chyoki Gyatso Institute of Buddhist Studies.

Zangdopelri Lhakhang

Zangdopelri is known as the 'Celestial Abode of Guru Rinpoche'. The three-storey temple set in the middle of the town is embellished with the work of master Bhutanese artisans. It serves as a spiritual refuge for locals to pray, make offerings and perform religious activities. You can often find elderly Bhutanese circumambulating the Zangdopelri. Its intricate frescos and beautiful statues are truly a sight to behold.

The architecture of Zangdopelri Lhakhang perfectly reflects its heavenly name

Trashigang

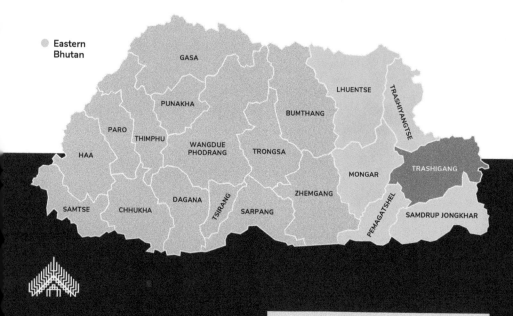

Eastern Bhutan

GASA
PUNAKHA
PARO
THIMPHU
HAA
WANGDUE PHODRANG
LHUENTSE
TRASHIYANGTSE
BUMTHANG
TRONGSA
MONGAR
TRASHIGANG
DAGANA
TSIRANG
ZHEMGANG
SAMTSE
CHHUKHA
SARPANG
PEMAGATSHEL
SAMDRUP JONGKHAR

Trashigang is popularly known as 'The Jewel of the East'. It is the largest district with three sub-districts and fifteen villages, with altitudes ranging from 600 m to over 4000 m. The largest river in Bhutan, Drangme Chhu, flows through this district.

Trashigang is also at the junction of the East-West Highway with road connections to Samdrup Jongkhar and the Indian state of Assam. Furthermore, Trashigang is the principal marketplace for the semi-nomadic people of Merak and Sakteng villages. These indigenous tribes speak their own dialects and have distinctive cultures. They have a unique dressing style that is different from the traditional Bhutanese *gho* and *kira*.

There is also a domestic airport in Trashigang known as Yonphulla Airport.

Attractions

- Trashigang Dzong
- Khaling National Handloom Development Centre
- Radhi Village
- Khardung Anim Dratshang
- Rangjung Woesel Choeling Monastery
- Gom Kora
- Merak Village

Trashigang Dzong

The dzong was founded according to the prophecy of Zhabdrung Ngawang Namgyal. In order to spread the Drukpa rule over the eight regions of eastern Bhutan, he directed the Trongsa governor, Chogyal Minjur Tempa, to subdue the local chief and build a dzong at the present site.

Trashigang Dzong was strategically built and you can only access it from the north through a narrow path. From the basement, the dzong rises to a height of five storeys at the central tower. It houses several temples, amongst which Dupthob Lhakhang is considered the most precious and sacred. It contains the statue of Thangthong Gyalpo — the great iron bridge builder of the Himalayan region.

From the dzong, you can see the calmly flowing river against the mountains. The stunning views make this place a paradise for photographers.

One of the largest ancient fortresses in Bhutan, overlooking the beautiful lush green valleys

Radhi Village

Radhi village is renowned for its textile production, especially *bura* (raw silk). The village is also famous for its rice fields and weaving expertise. It is often known as the 'Rice Bowl of the East' because of its lush rice fields that supply most of the grains in the eastern parts of the country.

The village has a community of around 200 households where the people make a living from *bura* textiles during the off-agricultural seasons. All textiles produced in Radhi are made using the traditional backstrap loom and traditional dyes. Thus, Radhi village produces some of the highest quality raw silk textiles you can find anywhere in Bhutan.

Khardung Anim Dratshang

Khardung Anim Dratshang, also known as Thakcho Lunzang Choden Nunnery, was built as a Ranjung Woesel Choeling Monastery branch.

This captivating and beautiful nunnery situated at Radhi village is a prominent tourist attraction due to its strategic location and scenic view. You can often see elderly women performing religious activities for the well-being of all sentient beings. If you are interested to learn more about Buddhism, you can also stay overnight in the guesthouse next to the monastery to observe the nuns' lifestyle and daily rituals.

Rangjung Woesel Choeling Monastery

Rangjung Woesel Choeling Monastery was founded by Dungsey Garab Dorje Rinpoche in 1989. The monastery exists to provide a conducive space for the study of Buddhist dharma teachings as expounded in the Dudjom New Treasure lineage, and to carry out dharma activities for the benefit of the Buddhist community in Bhutan and abroad. It has a flourishing community with four retreat centres and more than three hundred nuns and monks.

Khaling National Handloom Development Centre

Khaling National Handloom Development Centre is situated between Samdrup Jongkhar and Trashigang and is easily accessible. A prominent feature of the centre is that it showcases traditional weaving and knitting of the unique Bhutanese textiles. It is also a great shopping destination if you're looking for Bhutanese handicraft or traditional clothes.

You can find more than 300 textile designs at Khaling National Handloom Centre

Gom Kora

The name Gom Kora or Gomphu Kora comes from a meditation cave where Guru Rinpoche used to meditate. *Gomphu* means 'meditation cave' and *kora* means 'circumambulation'. Gom Kora Temple is an ancient temple with strong cultural significance. Guru Rinpoche meditated here and left a body imprint on a rock, like the one in Kurjey Lhakhang in Bumthang.

The temple houses numerous sacred objects and relics such as a garuda egg, Guru Rinpoche's boot print, the footprint of his consort, Yeshe Tsogyal, hoofprint of Guru Rinpoche's horse and a phallus-shaped rock that belonged to Pema Lingpa.

Interestingly, you can also test your sin level at the passageway that leads from the cave to the side exit of the rock. You do this by climbing up the side of the rock, and they say that only the virtuous can make it.

Gom Kora Temple is a must-visit when you are in eastern Bhutan

Merak Village

Merak is a settlement in the far east of Bhutan, situated at an altitude of 3,500 m. The village inhabitants are semi-nomadic people known as Brokpas, 'highlanders'.

Merak and Sakteng were closed to foreigners until 2010 to protect the area's traditional culture from external influence. Previously, you could only access Merak through a two-day hike. With the road construction in 2012, visitors can now reach Merak village within three to four hours from Trashigang town even though the road is very rough.

The Brokpas were originally from the Tshona region in South Tibet, and they have resided in Bhutan for centuries. The Brokpa settlements are scattered around the village. The houses are usually a single storey built of stones with small windows.

The Brokpas have a very distinct culture with their own dialect and a unique outfit different from the traditional Bhutanese dress. The men wear a thick red wool coat called tshokan chuba. Meanwhile, women wear a red and white striped dress called shingkha, adorned with Tibetan amber, silver and gold. Both men and women also wear the shamo, black felted yak wool.

The highlanders sustain their livelihood by raising domestic animals such as yaks and sheep. Fermented yak cheese is a delicacy in the region. Brokpas either barter or sell their limited produce to procure other basic needs.

The Brokpa hat — that has what looks like five spider legs — helps to keep the rain away from their faces

Eastern Bhutan is a Shangri-la for landscape photographers

Trashiyangtse

Eastern Bhutan

GASA

PUNAKHA

PARO

THIMPHU

HAA

WANGDUE PHODRANG

LHUENTSE

BUMTHANG

TRASHIYANGTSE

TRONGSA

MONGAR

TRASHIGANG

DAGANA

TSIRANG

ZHEMGANG

SAMTSE

CHHUKHA

SARPANG

PEMAGATSHEL

SAMDRUP JONGKHAR

Trashiyangtse is one of the newest districts in the country. It spans 1,437 sq. km of subtropical and alpine forests. It was formerly part of the Trashigang district, but it was separated in 1992. Trashiyangtse is the perfect destination for nature and wildlife lovers. It's home to some of the country's most important protected areas, such as Kulong Chhu Wildlife Sanctuary, a part of Bumdeling Wildlife Sanctuary.

The district is immensely rich in flora and fauna and a melting pot of cultures with diverse indigenous dwellers that speak different languages. The region is also famous for its marvellous woodworking and paper-making skills.

Attractions

- Bumdeling Wildlife Sanctuary
- Chorten Kora
- Trashiyangtse Institute of Zorig Chusum
- Omba Ney

Chorten Kora

Chorten Kora stupa was built by Lama Ngawang Loday in 1740 and has a similar design as Nepal's Boudhanath Stupa. Lama Ngawang Loday took twelve years to construct the chorten with the help of his devotees from the eastern region.

Legend has it that a princess from Tawang, believed to have been a khando (dakini) agreed to be buried alive inside the chorten to meditate on behalf of all beings.

There are two interesting festivals held here every year: Dakpa Kora and Drukpa Kora. During Dakpa Kora, the Dakpa tribe from Arunachal Pradesh, a north-eastern state of India, visit Chorten Kora to circumambulate the chorten. On Drukpa Kora, people from all over eastern Bhutan visit the chorten to generate merits and watch the unfurling of the thongdrel.

Bumdeling Wildlife Sanctuary

The sanctuary was established in 1998 and consists of diverse flora and fauna with magnificent scenery, including alpine lakes and the Bumdeling valley. There are more than 300 bird species, 700 plant species and 42 types of animals, including exotic animals like the white-tailed eagles, snow leopards, royal Bengal tigers, barking deers, Himalayan black bears and red pandas.

The sanctuary also houses important historical and cultural sites such as Dechen Phodrang Lhakhang and Singye Dzong.

There is a popular Bhutanese film, 'Chorten Kora' that recounts the legends of the site

Omba Ney

Omba Ney is also known as the 'Taktsang of East Bhutan'. It is built on a cliff and located within the holy pilgrimage site of Omba Ney, where you can see the letter 'Om' on the face of the rock. It is one of the three unique holy places linked to Guru Rinpoche, the others being Aja Ney and Hungrel Ney, where you can see the letters 'Ah' and 'Hum', respectively.

Omba Ney is a popular trek in eastern Bhutan, traversing broadleaved forests, chir pine savannahs, sub-alpine pastures, agricultural areas and small quaint villages. You can complete the hike in three to six days at a moderate to very relaxed pace.

Trashiyangtse Institute of Zorig Chusum

Trashiyangtse Institute of Zorig Chusum was established in 1997 in eastern Bhutan, under the then National Technical Training Authority. The institute aims to preserve Bhutan's thirteen traditional arts and crafts and promote the skills amongst the Bhutanese youths. Aside from imparting those precious traditional skills to the youths, the institute also hopes to create job opportunities for the next generation.

In the institute, you can watch students hone their crafts and support their efforts by purchasing their handicrafts that are for sale at the shop.

Trashiyangtse Institute of Zorig Chusum provides training in 10 of the 13 traditional Bhutanese crafts

Students can either opt for a 2-year certification course or 6-year diploma course

Mongar

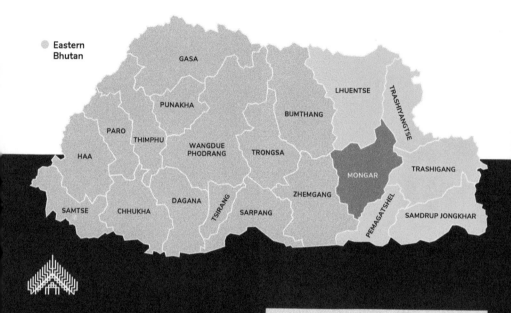

Eastern
Bhutan

GASA

PUNAKHA

LHUENTSE

TRASHIYANGTSE

BUMTHANG

PARO

THIMPHU

WANGDUE
PHODRANG

TRONGSA

HAA

MONGAR

TRASHIGANG

DAGANA

ZHEMGANG

PEMAGATSHEL

TSIRANG

SAMTSE

CHHUKHA

SARPANG

SAMDRUP JONGKHAR

The road approaching Mongar is one of
the most spectacular stretches in the
country. It passes over sheer cliffs, then
through beautiful fir forests and green
pastures. Travellers taking this route will
have opportunities to enjoy the bloom of
rhododendrons. If you are lucky, you can
even catch a glimpse of Gangkhar Puensum,
the tallest mountain in the country.

Mongar is one of the fastest developing
districts in eastern Bhutan. It covers an
area of 1,954 sq. km with steep slopes and
undulating surfaces.

The district is also famous for producing the
well-loved lemongrass spray that you find
everywhere in the country. The lemongrass
aroma is a smell that many travellers will
vividly remember even years after leaving
Bhutan.

Attractions

- Korila Pass
- Drametse Lhakhang
- Mongar Dzong
- Kilikhar Shedra
- Aja Ney

Mongar Dzong

Mongar Dzong was built in the 1930s to replace Zhongar Dzong. The dzong is located just above Mongar Town on a gentle sloppy hill.

The dzong was built at the site where the master architect saw a white stone shaped like a bowl. Thus it was formerly called Zhongar, 'white bowl'. You'll be charmed by the beautiful view from the dzong.

Korila Pass

En route to Mongar from Trashigang, you will cross Korila Pass at 2,450 m elevation. You will see a charming chorten, a mani wall and fluttering prayer flags at the pass. Expect to travel through beautiful coniferous forests along the journey.

At Korila Pass, you can also visit a small shop nearby to offer butter lamps for your safe journey ahead. Lighting butter lamps is a common spiritual practice for Bhutanese. When a Bhutanese lights a butter lamp, they offer prayers for all sentient beings. The act of offering butter lamps symbolises the offering of wisdom and light to dispel darkness and ignorance.

Aja Ney

Aja Ney, situated in Ngatsang village in Mongar district, is another sacred site located at an altitude of more than 3,500 m in eastern Bhutan. The ney (sacred site) was discovered by Guru Rinpoche when he meditated in the cave for three months. A rock that bears the inscriptions of 100 syllables of 'Ah' is said to have been imprinted there after Guru Rinpoche completed his meditation.

Kilikhar Shedra

Located 2 km from Mongar Town along the Trashigang-Mongar road lies a beautiful Buddhist temple built on a hilltop overlooking Mongar Valley. The official name of the temple is Lungtok Choekye Gatshel Shedra which roughly translates into 'Hilltop Garden of Religion'.

The main temple of Kilikhar Shedra is a replica of Punakha Maachen Lhakhang in Punakha Dzong. Due to the long distance, people from eastern Bhutan may not be able to go to Punakha easily. Hence, Kilikhar Shedra was built in Mongar for pilgrims in eastern Bhutan to receive blessings with the same spiritual satisfaction as having visited Punakha Maachen Lhakhang itself.

Drametse Lhakhang

Along the highway between Trashigang and Mongar lies a notable religious site known as Drametse Lhakhang. It was built by Ani (nun) Cheten Zangmo, the granddaughter of the famous treasure revealer, Terton Pema Lingpa, in the 16th century. Drametse means 'the peak where there is no enemy' or 'peak without enemy'.

The temple is deeply associated with Terton Pema Lingpa and the Peling tradition of Buddhism. It houses a wide range of sacred objects and serves as a source of spiritual inspiration to the people of Drametse and the neighbouring communities.

The remarkable Drametse Ngacham, a sacred dance, has been performed for almost five centuries, and its influence has spread throughout the country. The famous dance depicts 100 peaceful and wrathful deities — performed in tshechus — originated from Drametse.

Drametse Ngacham is so special that it was proclaimed a Masterpiece of the Oral and Intangible Heritage of Humanity by UNESCO in November 2005.

Drametse Festival takes place twice a year at Drametse Lhakhang, on the 1st and 10th month of the Bhutanese calendar.

Drametse Lhakhang is a key spiritual centre in eastern Bhutan

Lhuentse

Eastern Bhutan

GASA
LHUENTSE
TRASHIYANGTSE
PUNAKHA
BUMTHANG
PARO
THIMPHU
WANGDUE PHODRANG
TRONGSA
HAA
MONGAR
TRASHIGANG
ZHEMGANG
DAGANA
TSIRANG
PEMAGATSHEL
SAMTSE
CHHUKHA
SARPANG
SAMDRUP JONGKHAR

Lhuentse is one of the most isolated districts in Bhutan, located in the north-eastern part of the country. It is also the ancestral home of the monarchs and hosts a number of sacred sites in the country.

Lhuentse is famous for its distinctive textiles, which are considered to be amongst the best in the country. Women in this region are especially adept at weaving an extremely intricate patterned silk *kira* known as *kishuthara*.

Lhuentse also connects three major national parks in the country, Wangchuck Centennial Park in the north, Bumdeling Wildlife Sanctuary in the east and Thrumshingla National Park in the south.

Attractions

- Takila Guru Statue
- Pottery Farm at Gangzur Village
- Khoma Village
- Dungkar Nagtshang

Takila Guru Statue

One of the most popular attractions in Lhuentse is the 4.5 m statue of Guru Padmasambhava in Takila overlooking the entire valley of Tangmachu. The statue of Guru Padmasambhava in the form of Guru Nangsi Zilnon symbolises the subjugation of negative forces.

It is believed that the statue was built after the sacred prophecy of the great Terton Lerab Lingpa, who prophesied that, 'At one point of time, there will be a war of horses in Kurtoe Valley. To prevent the war, a statue of Guru Nangsi Zilnon shall be built'.

Pottery Farm at Gangzur Village

Gangzur village, about 2 km from Lhuentse town, is a small village consisting of 10 households. Lush green forest and spectacular mountains surround the village made up of traditional double storey houses. The pottery farm is well-known in the village, and you can observe skilled potters make earthen pots. This traditional craft serves as the main source of income for the people in Gangzur village.

Khoma Village

Khoma village is famous for their traditional weaving skills that has been passed on for generations. Their signature kishuthara textiles are highly sought-after all over the country. Kishuthara is generally used for kiras, but they can also be made into other products like bags, scarfs and table cloths. You can observe the exceptional weaving skills of the women as they create intricate designs and patterns.

Dungkar Nagtshang

The name 'Dungkar' originated from the physical shape of the land that resembles the shape of a conch shell. The house of Dungkar belongs to Trongsa Penlop, Jigme Namgyal, ancestor of the Wangchuck dynasty, the present royal family of Bhutan. The house sits against the backdrop of a towering mountain, overlooking the tiny Dungkhar village below.

There is also a temple, Dungkar Choeje Lhakhang, located in the village. The temple houses many sacred relics and treasures discovered by the famous treasure revealer, Terton Pema Lingpa, and great saint Desi Tenzin Rabgay.

The gigantic statue of Guru Padmasambhava in Lhuentse is surrounded by eight big and 108 small stupas

Pemagatshel district is currently still under development for tourism.

Eastern Bhutan

GASA

LHUENTSE

TRASHYANGTSE

PUNAKHA

BUMTHANG

PARO

THIMPHU

WANGDUE PHODRANG

TRONGSA

HAA

MONGAR

TRASHIGANG

ZHEMGANG

DAGANA

TSIRANG

SARPANG

PEMAGATSHEL

SAMTSE

CHHUKHA

SAMDRUP JONGKHAR

Pemagatshel

Pemagatshel translates to 'Lotus Garden of Happiness'. The district is notable for its artists, weavers and religious traditions such as folk dances and music. The tshechu festival in the district is also a popular attraction. Ausa, a famous folk song of the district, is sung on special occasions such as the departure of family members, relatives or friends.

The region is also known for its locally made sweet, known as tsatsi buram. The sweet is made from the abundant sugarcane that grows in Pemagatshel district and is well-liked throughout the country.

Itinerary recommendations

If you have only four days in Bhutan, you may explore the capital city, Thimphu and the picturesque Paro district. That way, you'll be able to check out some of the top attractions of Bhutan, such as **Buddha Dordenma**, **Tashichho Dzong**, and **National Memorial Chorten**.

Visit **Simply Bhutan** to learn more about Bhutanese culture and traditions. Print your personalised stamps at **Bhutan Postal Museum**. If you are an animal lover, you may also include a visit to the **Motithang Takin Preserve** to see the unique national animal of Bhutan.

Depending on how much time you have, you might be able to squeeze in a day trip to Punakha to see the magnificent **Punakha Dzong** and the famous **Chimi Lhakhang**. Stop over at **Dochula Pass** for the spectacular views of the Himalayas.

For the third day, hike up to the iconic **Taktsang Monastery.** A trip to Bhutan is said to be incomplete without a visit to Taktsang Monastery. Spend the remaining time exploring the charming town of Paro, where there are many handicraft shops and restaurants. You can also admire the night view of **Rinpung Dzong**.

Visit the majestic Rinpung Dzong in Paro

One week in Bhutan will allow you to explore Bhutan at a relaxed pace. You will have more time to admire the Bhutanese culture and visit more places. With seven days in Bhutan, you can spend two days in **Thimphu**, two days in **Punakha** and a day (or two) in **Paro**. You can also opt for an overnight trip to visit the small quaint **Haa** district.

To have a good understanding of Bhutanese culture and heritage, visit the **Royal Textile Academy, Simply Bhutan, Folk Heritage Museum** and **Jungshi Handmade Paper Factory**. Admire the grandeur of Bhutanese architecture at **Tashichho Dzong** and see the largest sitting Buddha statue in the kingdom at **Buddha Dordenma**.

In Punakha, you can visit all the major attractions, including **Punakha Dzong,** **Chimi Lhakhang** and **Khamsum Yulley Namgyal Chorten**. For a memorable experience, include some **whitewater rafting activity** (fees apply). Remember to book the activity in advance if you are keen to experience whitewater rafting.

If you have ample time in Paro, visit **Kyichu Lhakhang**, one of the oldest monasteries in Bhutan. For an authentic Bhutanese experience, opt for a homestay or arrange for a hot stone bath (fees apply) experience. Of course, hiking up to **Taktsang Monastery** should be on your itinerary.

If you go to Haa, stop by **Chele La Pass** to admire the fluttering prayer flags and magnificent Himalayan range. Visit **Juneydrak Hermitage** and **Shelkar Drak**. Embrace the untouched beauty and serenity of the least populated valley in Bhutan.

Catch the glorious sunrise at Chele La Pass

A good ten days in Bhutan will bring you deeper into the country. If you have ten days in the kingdom, you can travel further to **Bumthang**, the spiritual heartland of Bhutan. In addition to the 7-day itinerary to **Thimphu, Paro** and **Punakha**, you will be able to experience the charm of **Phobjikha Valley**.

You'll have an opportunity to check out the beautiful **Gangtey Goemba**, and see the sacred **black-necked cranes** (November to February). Phobjikha Valley in **Wangdue Phodrang** is a perfect destination for nature lovers. If you enjoy walking, opt for the **Gangtey Nature Trail** and traverse through the Bhutanese villages.

En route to Bumthang, you may also stop by **Trongsa** to see the largest fortress in

Bhutan, **Trongsa Dzong**. A visit to Trongsa will allow you to better understand the highly respected royal family of Bhutan.

You can spend two days in Bumthang to visit **Kurjey Lhakhang, Jambay Lhakhang** and **Jakar Dzong**. A must-visit in Bumthang is the popular **Mebar Tsho (Burning Lake)**. There, you can learn about the interesting history behind the lake and even meditate. Check out **Bumthang Brewery and Cheese Factory** to get a taste of the local cheese.

With more days in Bhutan, you can also do other short trails, such as the popular **Bumdra Trek**. Camping overnight in the wilderness will definitely make your trip to Bhutan an exciting and unforgettable one. Pamper yourself with a **hot stone bath** after the trek.

The lush green Bumthang valley in central Bhutan

With two weeks in Bhutan, consider a trekking tour such as **Jomolhari Loop** to explore the breathtaking Himalayan mountains. Otherwise, you can book an **east to west Bhutan tour**, exploring the less beaten paths. Your journey will begin from **Samdrup Jongkhar** in the eastern district, and you will alight at **Guwahati Airport** in India instead of Paro Airport. Do note that you will have to book your own visa for India (if required) should you opt for this arrangement. From Guwahati Airport, you will travel around 3 hours to reach Samdrup Jongkhar district in Bhutan.

Eastern Bhutan has a pristine environment that is unparalleled in the kingdom. It's a destination for those who want to experience the charm and simplicity of rural life — a magical place that exudes calmness, beauty and peace.

From Samdrup Jongkhar, you will visit **Trashigang**, the 'Jewel of the East', an incredibly picturesque district.

You'll be able to interact with the Brokpas to understand their unique culture, customs and traditions. Visit popular attractions in eastern Bhutan such as **Gom Kora, Khaling National Handloom** and **Trashigang Dzong**. You can also hunt for the elusive yetis in Trashigang!

Thereafter, you can visit the other eastern districts such as **Trashiyangtse, Mongar** and **Lhuentse**. At Trashiyangtse, check out **Chorten Kora** and **Trashiyangtse Institute of Zorig Chusum** to learn about the 13 traditional arts and crafts of Bhutan. Offer a butter lamp at **Korila Pass** and visit the **Drametse Lhakhang** in Mongar. Take a day trip to Lhuentse to visit **Khoma village** and **Takila Guru Statue**.

From Mongar, you'll travel back to **Bumthang** in central Bhutan and eventually make your way to **Punakha, Thimphu** and **Paro** in western Bhutan. Check out the 7-day itinerary for attractions in those districts.

Beautiful views from Khaling National Handloom Development Centre

Bhutan
Essentials

Where to go shopping in Bhutan?

For the best Bhutanese products, visit The Craft Gallery, a store located in Thimphu town. The two-storey shop showcases some of the finest crafts by the local artisans. The Craft Gallery is a project of the Gyalyum Charitable Trust, initiated by Queen Mother Sangay Choden Wangchuck. Aside from promoting authentic quality Bhutanese products, the gallery also strives to provide a sustainable income stream for the artisans. Thus, by purchasing from the gallery, you directly contribute to the cause of various non-profit organisations and local artisans. You can find all kinds of local products such as shawls, honey, embroidery goods, jewellery and textiles. It's definitely a great place for one-stop souvenir shopping if you're planning to grab some souvenirs for friends and family back home.

Thimphu and Paro are the best places to quench your shopping thirst. You will find exquisite *kiras* and *ghos*, colourful masks, prayer flags, handwoven textiles, Buddhist paintings, and traditional handicrafts in most of the shops. You can also buy popular products such as honey, cordyceps, wooden products or lemongrass spray.

The Craft Gallery

Address: Norzin Lam 3, Thimphu, Bhutan (Opposite Bhutan Development Bank Limited [BDBL]; behind Department of Revenue and Customs [DRC] and the Duty Free Shop)

Opening hours:
Monday to Saturday
9am - 5pm (Mar to Oct)
9am - 4pm (Nov to Feb)

Bhutan Natural

Address: Paro town
(located near Chhoeten Lhakhang)

Opening hours:
Monday to Sunday
9am - 5pm

What can you buy from Bhutan?

Bhutanese textiles are a reminder of the rich Bhutanese culture

Cordyceps

Cordyceps is a popular gift from Bhutan

Lemongrass Spray

The multipurpose spray has a long-lasting aroma

The K5 Blended Scotch Whiskey is the first and finest blend of whiskey in Bhutan. It is named 'K5' to commemorate the coronation of the fifth King of Bhutan, Jigme Khesar Namgyel Wangchuck, in 2008. The special recipe of the whiskey was discovered in an old distillery in the Himalayan mountains and assembled by distillers in Gelephu. K5 whiskey was produced under the Bhutanese Army Welfare Project.

If you're an alcohol lover, you can check out Drunken Yeti Bar. It's a new bar located opposite City Mall, Thimphu. Many claim that they serve the best cocktails in town. Alternatively, you can go to popular Mojo Park located right opposite Changlimithang Stadium in Thimphu to grab a drink and listen to live music.

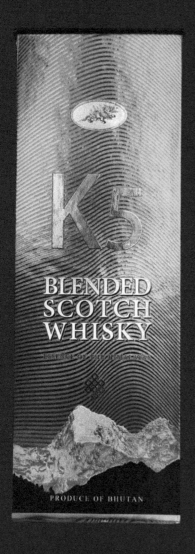

Bhutanese handicrafts are wonderful souvenirs for friends and family

Sacred wooden masks are great unique decors for your home

Frequently Asked Questions (FAQs)

01.

Is the Internet available and reliable?

Most of the hotels offer free wifi, but some may be limited to the lobby area. Internet connection is generally good in bigger districts like Thimphu, Paro, Trongsa and Bumthang. Some remote valleys may have intermittent connectivity. You should purchase a SIM card upon arrival in Bhutan if you want to have an Internet connection.

02.

Where can I purchase a mobile sim card?

There are two network providers in Bhutan. B-Mobile (Bhutan Telecom), which is government-owned, and a private company, Tashi Cell. You can purchase a tourist SIM card from the airport, mobile operator office, or any authorised dealer in larger towns like Paro and Thimphu. You will need your passport copy and 200 Ngultrum (~3 USD). You might want to get an extra few hundred Ngultrum, especially if you want to call abroad or use the Internet. You can load your balance by buying recharge vouchers, which comes in Nu. 50 to Nu. 500 values. The vendor can assist you with the SIM card and data plan activation.

03.

Can I withdraw money from the ATM?

You may not always be able to withdraw any money from the local ATMs. It is advisable for you to bring along cash for out-of-pocket expenses.

04.

Can I make payments with credit cards?

Credit cards are not commonly accepted in Bhutan yet. You should bring along cash for payment. Most places accept payment in major foreign currencies.*

05.

Can I exchange currency in Bhutan?

Yes, aside from the airport, you can also exchange for Ngultrum at the Bank of Bhutan in Thimphu and Paro. However, they only accept 12 major currencies.* It's better to bring larger denominations for exchange.

06.

Do I need to tip in Bhutan?

Tipping is purely a personal affair. It is not the Bhutanese culture to tip. However, if you would like to tip your tour guide or driver as a gesture of gratitude, you may do so.

07.

What should I wear?

You should dress modestly, such as long sleeve shirts, full-length pants, and shoes, especially when visiting the dzongs, temples, or monasteries. If you are wearing a T-shirt, you will be required to wear a cardigan or jacket over it when visiting those places. You are also not allowed to wear a hat or cap inside the temples or monasteries.

As a general tip, it would be wise to always have a jacket with you when travelling in Bhutan, as you will be charting through different altitudes. Some valleys can be colder than others.

08.

Do I need to purchase travel insurance?

It is not mandatory to purchase travel insurance, but we highly encourage you to get one, especially during turbulent times. Travel insurance will protect you in the event of any unexpected or unforeseen circumstances.

Tips

*Bhutan only accepts 12 major foreign currencies for exchange: U.S. Dollar, Pound Sterling, Euro, Japanese Yen, Swiss Franc, Hong Kong Dollar, Canadian Dollar, Danish Krone, Norwegian Krone, Swedish Krona, Australian Dollar and Singapore Dollar.

Dos

- Dress conservatively (no jeans or revealing clothing) while visiting religious sites and government offices.

- Bring along some earplugs if you are a light sleeper, as there may be dogs barking sometimes.

- Remove your headgear and take off your footwear before entering the temples.

- Maintain silence in heritage or religious sites.

- Always walk in a clockwise direction when circumambulating a chorten, stupa, or prayer wheels.

- Always carry and produce valid travel documents when required.

- Purchase insurance in case of any unforeseen circumstances.

- Be responsible for your own waste and dispose of them appropriately.

- Follow traffic rules and use designated zebra crossings for your own safety.

- Always get advice from your tour guide if you are unsure of cultural appropriateness.

- Be respectful of the members of the royal family as the Bhutanese hold them in high esteem.

- Use both hands when receiving or giving any objects to be polite.

- Ask for permission if you'd like to take photographs of the locals.

- It's customary for Bhutanese to make a small donation at a monastery or temple. You can also offer a small donation should you wish to do so.

- If you purchase a *thangka* (Buddhist painting) or other religious artefacts, keep the receipts to present to customs officers upon departure.

Don'ts

- Refrain from touching any murals, paintings or objects in the temples.

- Refrain from pointing at sacred items, deities or paintings. Instead, use an open-palm gesture with your palm facing up.

- Do not sit with your feet pointed towards anyone older than you or at any Buddhist deities or statues.

- Carrying and using drones in Bhutan is strictly prohibited.

- Refrain from taking photographs or filming in restricted areas. Always check with your guide if you are unsure whether it's permissible.

- Refrain from feeding any animals that you encounter.

- Washing, swimming, or throwing objects into lakes or rivers are forbidden.

- Instead of handing out money or gifts, you are encouraged to form more authentic interactions and friendships with the locals.

- The exporting of antiques or any rare cultural artefacts out of Bhutan is prohibited. A permit from the Department of Antiquities is required.

- Bhutanese have a deep reverence for their religion, the royal family and the chief abbot. Refrain from passing any negative comments as it's considered very disrespectful.

Your Ultimate Bhutan Checklist

If you are travelling to Bhutan for the first time, it is natural to feel excited yet anxious, not knowing what to expect of this beautiful kingdom. This packing checklist will help you ease your anxiety and get ready for what might just be your most memorable trip ever!

Clothing

- Long trousers/pants
- T-shirts or long-sleeved shirts
- Cardigan or jacket
- Underwear
- Down jacket/windbreaker
- Sandals or flip flops
- Comfortable shoes
- Thick socks
- Hat
- Sunglasses
- Glasses

Electronics and accessories

- Lightweight backpack
- Camera
- International travel adaptor
- Water bottle
- Mobile phone
- Charger

Winter season extras

- Sweaters
- Warm jacket
- Winter coat
- Thermal innerwear
- Scarf
- Wool socks

Health and well-being

- Hand sanitiser
- Masks
- Motion sickness pills
- Sunscreen lotion
- Insect repellent
- Lip balm
- Toiletries
- Ear plugs
- Your personal medical kit

Important

- Passport
- Approved visa for Bhutan
- Copies of passport and visa
- Identity card
- Flight ticket
- Money for exchange
  * Check out FAQs page for the 12 major currencies accepted in Bhutan

Useful Websites

Bhutan Tour Operator and Drukair's Representative

Druk Asia
60 Albert St, #12-03/04
OG Albert Complex,
Singapore 189969
+65 6338 9909
hello@drukasia.com
www.drukasia.com

Royal Bhutan Airlines (Drukair)

www.drukair.com

Tourism Council of Bhutan

www.bhutan.travel

Treks in Bhutan

www.bhutantreks.com

Emergency Numbers

Ambulance
112

Police
113

Fire brigade
110

Bhutanese Products

Bhutan Natural
www.bhutannatural.com

The Craft Gallery
www.bhutancrafts.com

Cordycep Sinensis
www.cordycepssinensis.org

You can remain connected to your loved ones while you are in Bhutan. Bhutan's country code is **975**. To call Bhutan from overseas, dial either 00975 or +975 (for mobile phones), followed by the phone number.

Independent News Oulet

Daily Bhutan
www.dailybhutan.com

BHUTAN ESSENTIALS

Basic Conversational Phrases in Dzongkha

Hello

Kuzuzangpo la

How are you?

Chey ga dey bay yue?

What is your name?

Ming ga chi mo?

I am fine

Nga lesom bay ra yue

My name is ...

Nga gi ming ... in

What is this?

Ani ga chi mo?

Thank you

Kadinchey la

How much is it?

Teru ga tey chi mo?

I love you

Nga chey lu ga

What time is it?

Chutse ga dem chi ya si?

Where are you from?

Chhoey ga tey lay mo?

Nice to meet you

Nga chey da chebay sem ga yi

How old are you?

Kay lo gadem chi ya si? (formal)
Chey gi lo gadem chi mo? (informal)

See you again

Log jay gay

Basic Conversational Phrases in Dzongkha

Do you understand?

Haa goi ga?

I don't understand Dzongkha

Nga Dzongkha mishey

Can you speak English?

Chey English lap chu ga?

Good morning

Doba delek

Where is the toilet?

Chhabsa ga ti mo?

Good afternoon

Nima delek

I want to go to_____

Nga _____ na jo ni

Good night

Zimcha delek

Let's go back to the hotel

Hotel na log jo gay

I'm sick

Nga nau mey

Can you help me?

Nga lu charo chi bay na mae?

Where is the hospital?

Menkhang ga tey in na?

Congratulations/Good luck

Tashi delek

Roger that

Las la or laso la

You will hear a lot of 'la' at the end of sentences when a Bhutanese speaks. The 'la' in Bhutan is not the same as the 'lah' commonly heard in the Singaporean or Malaysian slang. Using 'la' at the end of a sentence in Bhutan is a sign of respect.

It is delicious

Zhim tok tok du

May I take a photo?

Par chi taab ga?

Less spicy, please

Ema nu shu zhu gay la

Can I pay by credit card?

Credit card na pay bay tubga?

More spicy, please

Ema mum zhu gay

May I have the bill, please?

Bill zhu gay la?

Where is the money exchange?

Teru sosa gatey in na?

How long will it take?

Dutse gadem chi go wong ga?

Is there wifi?

Wifi yue ga?

Is it far?

Tha ring sa in na?

What's the wifi password?

Wifi password gachi mo?

Please wait a moment

Ah tsi tsi zhu na

See you tomorrow

Naba chey gae

No problem

Khe mi

Basic Conversational Phrases in Dzongkha

Yes, that's okay	**I feel so happy**
Khe min du	Nga sem ga yi
Not okay/not good	**I love this place**
Layzom min du	Sa cha ga tok to du or sa cha di na ga way
I don't want	**I'm feeling tired**
Nga mi zhu	Nga wu duk chi
I don't like it	**I love Bhutan**
Nga mi ga way	Nga Drukgyal kap gai
It's nice	**I miss Bhutan**
Ja chi chi	Nga Bhutan drenmae
That's fun	**I am hungry**
Trowa du	Toh kay chi
That's very good	**I am full**
Layzom ee mae	Pho dang si

Travellers' Tales

Travellers' Tales features exclusive Bhutan journeys by travellers from different walks of lives. Each of these travellers has embarked on a unique Bhutan journey of their own. Some of them have gone beyond their holiday and set roots in Bhutan, built a family with the Bhutanese or simply keep going back for more of the Bhutan charm!

Lester V. Ledesma

"Bhutan has visibly modernised through the years."

When did you first set foot in Bhutan?

My first visit to Bhutan was in July 2012. A friend I hadn't talked to in a while contacted me to ask if I was interested in joining a media trip to Bhutan.

What was your first impression of the country?

Paro Airport had all the atmosphere of a sleepy provincial airport, except that it was surrounded by lovely landscapes and pollution-free air. I could see the hillsides and the traditional wooden houses around the runway and thought this place was like nowhere I've been. I was itching to bring out my camera and shoot.

Compare your first visit to your most recent visit. How do you think Bhutan has changed?

Bhutan has visibly modernised through the years. Back in 2012, kids wore their ghos and kiras on the streets. Everyone watched local movies in the theatres. People didn't know who Iron Man was, but I remember watching a UFC match on the TV screen at a restaurant. In the bigger towns these days, the young ones wear western attire outside of school, and everyone has an Internet connection. Also, things are a bit more commercial now, especially in Paro which has a bigger tourism infrastructure. There are more hotels and international restaurants too. The countryside, however, remains timeless as ever.

What are your hopes and aspirations for Bhutan?

I really believe in the Gross National Happiness philosophy, and I hope that the Bhutanese can manage sustainable development without sacrificing their values and culture.

What are some qualities or traits that you admire about the Bhutanese?

The Bhutanese are deeply spiritual and are well-grounded in Buddhist values. They're not materialistic, and they don't sweat the small stuff. I've never seen an angry Bhutanese; they're very accepting of people no matter how strange they may be. And they have the sweetest, most genuine smiles.

Which is your favourite place in Bhutan?

Merak was amazing and truly off the beaten path — it's a pity I didn't spend enough time there. A place like that is the reason I became a photographer. So much to discover, so many stories to unwrap. And the landscapes are just breathtaking. Also, I wanna see the yeti.

Thimphu is fascinating to me because this is often where the outside world first shows its influence on the Bhutanese. I love watching the mix of modern and traditional elements as they clash, co-exist or just blend together. Also, being in Thimphu is a good reminder that you can have a relatively urban life with modern conveniences without having to live at a fast pace.

Award-winning writer and photographer Lester V. Ledesma (www.lesterledesma.com) has covered the world for a long list of local and international publications. Based in Singapore, he often organises PhotoTreks photography workshop tours in Bhutan. He has a penchant for subjects that involve cultural immersion, history, heritage and food. He also loves Red Panda Beer in Bhutan.

Shooting drayang performers at Paro

What are some of your most memorable experiences in Bhutan?

When travelling through Bhutan, I often asked the locals about their definitions of happiness, and their answers always put me to shame. They're not the least bit selfish. Happiness for them is most often connected to the well-being of those around them.

There was one night that I vividly remember. I was drinking whiskey with my guide on the balcony of our hotel in Punakha when the quiet evening was interrupted by the sound of a scream coming from a nearby hill. We then heard the *dungchen* (horns), and saw a huge fire light up the hilltop. It was so strange; even my guide had no idea what it was. The next day, we were told it was a funeral ritual for someone who had died prematurely. The sound and the fire were meant to scare the deceased's soul away so it wouldn't linger in the land of the living.

The first time I covered a *tshechu* was really memorable too. It was at Kurjey Lhakhang; the sights, sounds and smells of this fascinating event came to me all at once. It was sensory overload. There was so much to take in that I panicked and started shooting in a frenzy. I had to hit the pause button and dig deep into my training as a photojournalist, so that I could cover the event in a rational manner and tell a balanced story of it. I evaluated the situation and had to focus only on the things I needed to get my story. To this day, that experience is a reminder to me to always be mindful of the story I'm covering and not lose myself in it.

How would you describe Bhutan to your friends?

It's a place up in the Himalayas that is a world of its own. Bhutan is blessed with so much spirituality and culture that you can't help but live and breathe it.

How many times have you travelled to Bhutan?

8 times.

Any other thoughts/comments?

Despite my many visits to Bhutan, I never tire of this land. My mind feels at rest whenever I am there despite the fact that it is my work as a photojournalist and travel guide that brings me over. I hope someday to adopt the generosity and spirituality that embodies the Bhutanese way of life.

Posing with a Brokpa lady at Merak

Hanging prayer flags at Taktsang

Scott A. Woodward

"There is no other place on earth like enigmatic Bhutan. Its natural light is soft and golden, and the prayer-flag-strewn, snowcapped-mountain vistas are simply astounding."

When did you first set foot in Bhutan?

My first trip to Bhutan was in February 2008; I visited to document the nation's first-ever democratic election. For as long as I can remember, I'd fantasised about travelling to Bhutan, and this opportunity to photograph the country and its citizens during this historic event was one that I will always remember.

How do you think the country has changed over the decade?

I feel like Bhutan has done an impressive job of preserving its soul despite the universal creep of modernisation. Certainly the capital Thimphu is busier with automobile traffic now than it was a decade ago — and you observe less traditional dress being worn by the young people than during my first visit more than 13 years ago — but the spirit of the nation, its devotion to Buddhism, and its commitment to cultural conservation proudly endures.

What was your first impression of the country?

I recall being struck by the nation's sensational mixture of the stunning, rugged countryside, centuries-old architecture, vibrant and colourful culture, and the genuinely kind and welcoming Bhutanese whom I encountered everywhere.

What are your hopes and aspirations for Bhutan?

Bhutan is a nation at a crossroads, aiming to preserve its rich cultural heritage while still cautiously opening itself up to the world. My sincere hope is that the nation will continue its sustainable travel doctrine and maintain its high value, low impact travel philosophy in an effort to avoid the crush of over-tourism that plagues so many of Bhutan's neighbours.

At the pristine Jimi Langsto Lake

Riding across the country with my father and brother

What are some qualities or traits that you admire about the Bhutanese?

The Bhutanese are extremely proud of their history and cultural identity. They are deeply spiritual, thoughtful and peaceful. Furthermore, in all my experiences, they are incredibly warm, genuine and generous. The Bhutanese are beautiful people with whom you will certainly build lifelong friendships.

What are some of your most memorable experiences in Bhutan?

I have travelled to Bhutan eight times in the last dozen years, and each visit has provided me with new friendships and countless rich remembrances. However, the most memorable experience I've had in Bhutan was riding Royal Enfield motorcycles across the country with my father and brother. There is a Buddhist proverb that declares, "It is better to travel well than to arrive." This seems like an apt metaphor for riding a motorcycle in Bhutan. Our 11-day father & sons ride through the beautiful kingdom afforded us the opportunity to explore the mystical nation on two wheels, to visit so

Embracing the lush green valleys of Trongsa

many beautiful places, to meet so many interesting people and to have so many truly unique and unforgettable experiences together. And we were lucky enough to share it with our thoughtful and considerate guides, all of whom worked tirelessly to make our adventure a reality while becoming our friends along the journey. It was a dream trip for my family and I — a once-in-a-lifetime opportunity to breathe the rarified air of the 'Land of the Thunder Dragon' and to traverse the rugged and beautiful nation in the saddles of motorcycles. But more importantly, it was a chance to do this together as father and sons in one of the most special places on earth.

Which is your favourite place in Bhutan?

Enveloped by the Indian plains to the south and the mountainous Tibetan regions of China to the north, Bhutan is cradled deep in the creases of the soaring Himalayas. It is home to breathtaking natural topography and disparate climatic regions. Trekking through the Himalayan mountains was one of the most exhilarating experiences I had in Bhutan — and our snowy campsite at the spectacular frozen Jimi Langsto Lake (3,880 m) was one of my favourite places to visit in the kingdom.

How would you describe Bhutan to your friends?

There is no other place on earth like enigmatic Bhutan. Its natural light is soft and golden, and the prayer-flag-strewn, snowcapped-mountain vistas are simply astounding. Friendly locals in traditional Bhutanese dress fill bustling city markets while smiling monks in flowing maroon robes inhabit the ancient monasteries that dot the rugged countryside.

Scott A. Woodward is a Canada-born, Singapore-based highly distinguished photographer. He calls his photographic style "Choose Your Own Adventure Photography" after the books he used to read as a child. Scott has spent nearly 25 years living and shooting across Asia-Pacific and around the world. Browse Scott's portfolio at www.scottawoodward.com and follow him on Instagram at @iamscottawoodward

Admiring Taktsang Monastery, one of the most sacred sites in Bhutan

Karen Lim

"Bhutan is a lost paradise on earth!"

When did you first set foot in Bhutan?

I first set foot in Bhutan in August 2017.

Why did you choose Bhutan as your travel destination?

I have wanted to travel to the Himalayas since my teens but never found the opportunity to do so. Bhutan was on my list for 10 years, but it wasn't the first Himalayan destination I wanted to travel to. I had wanted to go to Tibet first but found it too much of a hassle to go there. Then I realised that Singapore had direct flights to Bhutan, so I chose to head to Bhutan first.

What was your first impression of the country?

My first impression was that it is a mysterious place that is totally out of the world. The people and architecture seem to be from another time and place altogether. It is almost like being transported to a different era.

What are some of your most memorable experiences in Bhutan?

I think it was the car rides. Journeying to other districts and watching the meandering valleys covered with pine trees and cypress trees. I love going up mountain passes because it is the fastest and simplest way to see one of the most beautiful views without having to trek for days. When I first had a taste of their national dish, ema datsi, I was truly surprised and really enjoyed it. It left an impression on me. I still enjoy it today, but nowadays, I prefer the spinach, mushroom or potato versions, with a bit of chilli. I also love their ezay (chilli pastes) and goen hogay — cucumber salad with chilli and crumbled cheese. Their vegetables are very fresh and a delight to eat.

What are some qualities or traits that you admire about the Bhutanese?

What I really admire about them is their humility, compassion and willingness to help. Many Bhutanese I know are extremely helpful and will go beyond their means to assist. Compassion for all beings is also a trait that they have grown up with, and it is visible in many things that they do.

With my Bhutanese husband, Ngawang, in Bhutan

At Ta Chog Lhakhang located along the Paro-Thimphu Highway

Which is your favourite place in Bhutan?

Phobjikha Valley is my favourite place so far. The valley is extremely wide, and it's possible to capture the beauty of the surroundings from different spots in the valley. Watching the black-necked cranes there is also a delightful experience and never fails to disappoint. A short hike through the pine tree forest is also a good way to experience the valley.

Who is the most interesting person you have met in Bhutan so far?

It is most definitely His Majesty the King, Jigme Khesar Namgyel Wangchuck. I met him at Paro Tshechu, which he visits almost every year. We only had a short conversation, but it was a very insightful and enlightening one for me.

Pre-wedding shoot in Bhutan

In traditional wear at Punakha Dzong

What advice do you have for solo female travellers to Bhutan?

Bhutan is one of the safest countries in the world for solo female travellers, so you can travel there without worrying too much. If you want to explore the nightlife or go out to town at night, ask your guide to go with you in case you don't know your way back. Also, dinners at your hotel are included in the daily package, so if venturing out is not something you want to do, you can always have a decent and good meal at the hotel.

What have you discovered about yourself after travelling to Bhutan?

I learned that travelling in Bhutan is about having an open mind and going with the flow. The weather may not be cooperative, or a local attraction may be closed on a particular day, so keep an open mind that things may change at the last minute due to unforeseen circumstances. This is how the Bhutanese get on with their lives too. They go with the flow because everything is transient, and things will go back to 'normal' eventually. Also, there's always a way to work things out in Bhutan, so even if you don't get to visit an attraction, your guide will arrange for something else.

How many times have you been to Bhutan?

I am grateful to have been able to live and work in Bhutan for more than a year after my first two trips there (one was a holiday, while the other as a media trainer). Altogether, I've been there 4 times so far. My husband and I intend to set up our home there eventually.

Josephine Sim

"You must visit Bhutan at least once in your lifetime!"

When did you first set foot in Bhutan?

My first visit to Bhutan was in November 2013. After watching a Taiwanese travel programme about the Taktsang 'Tiger's Nest' Monastery, I told myself that I must go to Bhutan someday.

What was your first impression of the country?

My first impression of Bhutan was that it was such a peaceful country. It was very different from the other countries that I have visited. Even the street dogs were so relaxed, just chilling and lying down. I even told some of my friends that if my next reincarnation is a dog, I will like to stay in Bhutan!

Which is your favourite place in Bhutan?

My favourite place in Bhutan is eastern Bhutan due to the awesome scenery and peaceful environment. I thought I was in Europe!

Why do you think people should visit Bhutan?

Bhutan is a great place to slow down our pace. The ambience and environment are so relaxing. In our busy city life, it feels like we are constantly in a rush for no good reason.

What is your most memorable experience in Bhutan?

My most memorable experience in Bhutan is hiking to Chumphu Nye 'Statue of Floating Goddess' in Paro. I was so amazed when the monk allowed me to test that the Buddha was floating by swiping a dollar under the Buddha's foot. Although the hike was tough, it was really worth it. I couldn't have done it without the help of my tour guide, Ugyen Tshewang and my driver, Sonam. I was really blessed to have both of them with me.

What is your favourite activity in Bhutan?

My favourite activity in Bhutan is to search for different bakery shops and try out all kinds of different food in Bhutan.

What are some food and eateries that you recommend in Bhutan?

The food in COMO Uma is really yummy. Aside from ema datshi, I also love their pizzas and momos! For the momos, I've tried both the Zombala outlets in Thimphu. They are a very famous local restaurant with raving reviews for their momos. The burger and ice-cream from Cloud 9 in Thimphu is also super delicious. If you want to unwind and chill, can check out Mountain Cafe in Paro.

What are some qualities or traits that you admire about the Bhutanese?

What I admire about the Bhutanese is the simple life that they lead. Simplicity is the cause for a happy life.

How would you describe Bhutan to your friends?

I always tell my friend that Bhutan is a must-visit place, at least once in our lifetime. Even though it can be expensive and the fare is comparable to flying to Europe, it is totally worth it!

How many times have you been to Bhutan?

I have been to Bhutan 3 times, and I am planning to visit Bhutan again and again. I really hope to visit Gasa, Druk Path Trek and eastern Bhutan again.

Josephine Sim is an avid traveller who believes that her purpose in this life is to travel the world. She has visited many countries and finds Bhutan to be different and a very unique country. She is a Tibetan Buddhist and enjoys visiting the different monasteries in Bhutan. Additionally, she also likes to visit places with historical architecture.

With my tour guide, Ugyen, and driver, Sonam, at Chumphu Nye

Beautiful landscapes at Gangtey

The huge Takila-Guru Statue in Lhuentse, eastern Bhutan

Chan Family

"A curious mix of modernity and tradition."

When did you first set foot in Bhutan?

Our first visit to Bhutan was a family holiday in April 2012. Emma was 9 and Christopher was 7.

What was your first impression of the country?

A: The sight of the mountains as we flew into Bhutan was unforgettable for me.

PC: The vastness of the land coupled with the warmth of the people.

E: While I do not remember my exact first impression, I do remember seeing the snowy mountaintops and that I was excited to walk on the apron at the airport.

C: I thought it was paradise! There was so much space to run around! Our first stop was an ancient iron suspension bridge. I remember feeling fear and exhilaration at the adventure of it all.

What are some of your most memorable experiences in Bhutan?

A: Seeing the rainbow over the Punakha valley was awe-inspiring.

PC: Sitting amongst the Bhutanese as they celebrated National Day in Thimphu is a precious memory. Also noteworthy are the scenic walks and Bhutanese picnics we had near Tango and Cheri mountains, just a short drive from Thimphu.

E: Driving to Phobjikha Valley to see the black-necked cranes; the mountainous roads were quite different. Being so high up that we were above rainbows was a new experience.

C: I love dogs, so seeing all the dogs — we call them Bhutan Specials — everywhere was a new experience for me. We even made a 'Dogs of Bhutan' photo folder.

Where is your favourite place in Bhutan?

A: I don't have one favourite place. Rather, I enjoy anytime I'm in the mountains of Bhutan.

PC: Bumthang — the apple trees, wildflowers, fields of buckwheat and the people we met there, all combined to make it my favourite place. Aside from that, the Royal Manas National Park is definitely the place to visit!

E: Junction bookstore in Thimphu! I love how the owner, Mui, has a heart for her community. Highly recommend it if you like dogs, books, coffee and supporting small businesses.

C: My favourite place in Bhutan is Thimphu. I prefer cities and cooler weather, making Thimphu the ideal location in Bhutan.

The Chans travelled in and out of Bhutan from 2012-2015 and moved to Bhutan for three years between 2015 and 2018. Adrian was in service to His Majesty, King Jigme Khesar Namgyel Wangchuck, as a leadership resource person. Poh Cheng homeschooled the kids, Emma and Christopher, due to Adrian's job requiring lots of travel. After spending three years in Bhutan, the Chans have relocated back to their home in Singapore.

Our first National Day Celebration in Changlimithang Stadium, Thimphu, in 2014

Our first visit to Dochula Pass in 2012

A family portrait in traditional Bhutanese attire taken in 2012

How would you describe your experience living in Bhutan?

A: It was very uplifting interacting with young people who are ready to help their country.

PC: A curious mix of modernity and tradition — that helped me realise the things I want to hold on to and to let go.

E: One of a kind and eye-opening. Being in Bhutan gave me a lot of time to reflect and learn more about myself.

C: Staying in Bhutan helped me develop my sense of self. Being around the many fun and energetic people I met and having the time to think helped shape my personality.

What was the hardest adjustment you had to make?

A: Having no comfort food was hard. However, this was somewhat offset by the sweetness of fresh organic vegetables and the variety of seasonal fruits (wild strawberries and kiwi), which I appreciated.

PC: Learning to winter-proof the house was an enlightening experience. Central heating isn't the norm in homes, and many traditional homes have a *bukhari* — traditional wood-burning stove — which makes for a cosy experience. The upside about winter in Bhutan is that travel on the roads is much more pleasant (no monsoon rains), and a lush retreat is available in the subtropical south.

E: This may be specific to us, but for me, the hardest adjustment to make was moving around all the time and not being able to set down roots.

C: Having to make new relationships was extremely tough. Bhutanese children of my age were mostly in school till 3 pm, and Saturday was a half school day for sports and community work. So most of my friends were working young adults!

What are some qualities or traits that you admire about the Bhutanese?

A: I admire how flexible they are about timing. They have named it BST, Bhutan Stretchable Time.

PC: The Bhutanese are such a diverse people, and I've been privileged to encounter some very deep thinkers who are friendly and ready to chat.

E: The Bhutanese are very easygoing and flexible, and I feel that I have adopted this mindset after living in Bhutan for 3 years.

C: I enjoy how the Bhutanese are so adventurous and ready to try new things.

What is the one thing you wish you could have brought back with you from Bhutan?

A: A mountain.

PC: Our landlady's garden with its beautiful flowers. I would also have liked some of the pear, plum and cherry blossom trees that lined some of their roads.

E: The dogs who lived in our neighborhood.

C: Raphie and Donut, the two dogs living at our compound.

How would you describe Bhutan to your friends?

A: Imagine a country against the side of the Himalayan slopes. It has a well-loved reigning king, a constitutional government, and it is intentional about balancing economic growth with Gross National Happiness.

PC: It's a unique place with beautiful mountains, hazardous roads, and rich cultural diversity.

E: I give them a geography lesson.

C: Bhutan is a landlocked Himalayan country, with beautiful glacial lakes and stories behind every mountain. It's hard to take a bad photograph there.

What was the most interesting thing you learned about the Bhutanese culture?

A: They are very spiritual in their outlook. Even the smallest things have meaning and they really value their natural resources.

PC: The people are generally very kind to each other and are always ready to share food, stories, and invite you to experience their community. This spirit of hospitality has deep roots in their geography. Before public transportation was made accessible, Bhutanese would travel days and weeks to visit other parts of the country. En route, travellers would depend on the kindness of strangers to host and house them — this legacy of the extended community still endures in modern Bhutan.

E: Bhutan is a very closely knit society where everyone knows each other. This was a bit of a culture shock coming from a big city where it's not uncommon not to know your neighbours. If you go out for a meal or groceries, you're bound to bump into someone you know! It has a sort of small-town feel to it, which was new to me.

C: The Bhutanese are very reverent towards the King. They love His Majesty with a daily devotion: proudly wearing badges with his portrait and purchasing prints of the royal family for display at their homes.

Any other comments or thoughts?

A: Bhutan's young generation and their King's dynamic leadership really gives me hope.

PC: There is such a stark contrast between Thimphu and southern or eastern Bhutan. You really need to travel off the usual tourist routes to appreciate the full complexity and diversity of the country.

E: Living in Bhutan at the time helped me realise that I enjoy stillness, and now it's a thing I actively search for.

C: Bhutan's biodiversity is really quite amazing; I really wish I learnt more about plants before moving there.

We really enjoyed exploring the different parts of the kingdom

We loved the weather in Punakha

Tian Chad

"Journey to Bhutan to heal your soul, get recharged and reframe your perspectives in life."

When did you first set foot in Bhutan?

My first visit to Bhutan was in December 2018. The weather was cool and ideal for travelling.

What was your first impression of the country?

I didn't expect much as I just wanted to explore a new travel destination. However, I didn't expect Bhutan to be so relaxing!

What are some of your most memorable experiences in Bhutan?

One of the most memorable experiences was when we explored Phobjikha Valley and saw a huge flock of black-necked cranes flying above us. It was a truly 'wow' experience! Another unforgettable experience was having a herbal stone bath at a local farmhouse. It was the perfect activity to pamper ourselves in the cold weather at night.

What are some qualities or traits that you admire about the Bhutanese?

I really admire the great faith that Bhutanese have in their life. I have learned a lot from the Bhutanese driver, Pema, who brought us around Bhutan and even climbed up to Tiger's Nest Monastery with us! I really like his philosophy of life on appreciating nature and being grateful — which somehow makes me a better person.

What was the most interesting thing you learned about the Bhutanese culture?

The approach to relationships between Bhutanese men and women is interesting. Bhutanese women are free to choose their life partners and can even stay in a live-in relationship without any formal wedding. There is no stigma around that, and it was really fascinating to me.

What were the most interesting sightings for you in Bhutan?

We were very lucky to see a group of beautiful langurs chilling on the trees, thanks to the sharp eyes of our awesome driver! Seeing the black-necked cranes was also very memorable. Last but not least, the view of Tiger's Nest was extra special too.

Which is your favourite place in Bhutan?

It's so hard to choose because I like all the places we visited in Bhutan. If I have to choose just one, I'll probably say Tiger's Nest because we hiked all the way up to the monastery. The beauty of the temple's architecture atop the mountain is awe-inspiring. The view before ascending the stairs to the monastery was absolutely beautiful — prayer flags fluttered against a backdrop of a waterfall and bridge.

Tian Chad is a photoblogger who loves to capture precious moments through his lenses and share them on his blog, TianChad.com. He likes to capture the genuine moments that he experiences during his travels and share them through his social media platform, @tianchad. He also produces travel videos to share the beauty of the countries he has visited. Check out his encounter with the beautiful black-necked cranes at Phobjikha Valley on his YouTube channel.

Behold the beauty of the ancient fortress, Punakha Dzong

In traditional Bhutanese dress, gho, at Punakha Dzong

Golden langurs chilling on the trees

How would you describe your travel experience and journey in Bhutan?

The trip to Bhutan was a journey to heal my soul and reframe my life perspectives. I did not expect the trip to be so relaxing that I got to recharge myself properly. I feel that the trip has also helped me become a better person in many ways.

What advice do you have for people who are contemplating travelling to Bhutan?

You don't have to worry about having insufficient time. Throughout the journey, I pretty much followed my own pace in exploring the beauty of Bhutan. Your tour guide will not rush you to travel from one place to another like the usual guided tours. You can enjoy the journey at your own pace and travel like a local!

What do you usually enjoy most when you travel abroad?

I enjoy learning about new cultures and experiencing things that I can never get in my hometown. Above all, it was a hassle-free process where everything — hotel, transportation, meals and tour guide — was well-arranged so that I was worry-free and could just enjoy the journey.

Any other comments or thoughts?

If you have been feeling down or lost your motivation to chase your dreams, take a break by visiting this beautiful country. Bhutan has a way of healing your soul. Trust me; you will feel recharged and pumped up and become your better self. Most importantly, get the right travel partner like Druk Asia to ease your travel experience.

Taking a selfie with the Bhutanese children

At the charming Thimphu town

Thimphu, the picturesque capital city of Bhutan

Darren Kee and Kate Ooi

"Spiritual immersion at Bhutan's sacred sites is something only a Neykor trip can offer."

When did you first set foot in Bhutan?

December 2019 was our very first trip to Bhutan.

Why did you choose Bhutan as your travel destination?

DK: I was searching for a different travelling experience and wanted to learn more about the Neykor tour.

KO: I had the simple thought of accompanying my husband but it ended up being a most memorable and remarkable experience with my loved one.

What was your first impression of the country?

DK: Very friendly people. Everything seemed slow-paced and calm.

KO: It felt like a trip back to nature. We were surrounded by awesome mountains and greeted by warm smiles from the friendly Bhutanese.

What were some of your most memorable experiences in Bhutan?

DK: Experiencing the simplicity of life, breathing clean air, observing the people's devotion and seeing the way nature is loved.

KO: Watching and getting insights on how Bhutanese live a simple yet happy and contented life. Also, visiting and practising meditation at various unique spiritual sites where there was an abundance of auspicious natural and spiritual energy.

Which is your favourite place in Bhutan?

DK: Burning Lake (Mebar Tsho). The serenity made me feel connected to my spirituality.

KO: Burning Lake. It felt so calm and soothing just sitting there. It recharged me physically and spiritually.

What are some qualities or traits that you admire about the Bhutanese?

DK: Extremely pleasant and simple people; no big urge for material desires.

KO: Simple and content with life which brings them happiness.

How was your Neykor tour experience in Bhutan?

DK: Enlightening. Although it was a little rushed and as such, we didn't have enough time to enjoy much of the scenery.

KO: Crossing mountains on car rides was thrilling and tiring, but at the same time, we felt a sense of accomplishment.

How would you describe Bhutan to your friends?

DK: It is among the top ten must-visit places in the world.

KO: Regardless of religion, Bhutan is a place to explore at least once in a lifetime.

What is your biggest takeaway from the Neykor trip?

DK & KO: Immersion is a key takeaway. We were able to revitalise and instil peace within ourselves. It reminds us to look at things differently and that there is more to life than what we see every day. There is so much to work on in ourselves and the rest of the world. We were also blessed to receive guidance and teachings from a passionate, outward-thinking modern monk, Khedrupchen Rinpoche. He shared about "applying compassion in business management and life" and the "RICH" (Respect, Integrity, Contentment, Humanity) philosophy which we adopted in our business and life as core values.

Darren Kee is an entrepreneur involved in the oil and gas industry. He has chased after business success and financial rewards for the past 25 years. He is now looking forward to a change of lifestyle to balance the different aspects of life, particularly the spiritual aspect, and deepen his understanding of the meaning of life. He hopes to learn more about Buddhism and practice Bodhicitta in his daily life by developing a genuine desire to help others in their lives.

Kate Ooi is a homemaker who loves nature's wonders. She has embarked on a journey to gain adventures.

Tea time at Lobesa Hotel, Punakha

Climbing up to the iconic Tiger's Nest

View of the beautiful Himalayan range

Robin Yap

"I must have been a Bhutanese in my past life as I feel like I'm back home each time I arrive in Bhutan."

When did you first set foot in Bhutan?

I first set foot in Bhutan in 2009 with a group of personal friends. During that trip, I was honoured to see the beginning of Buddha Dordenma's construction in Thimphu.

What was your first impression of the country?

There was an air of calmness that you can't experience anywhere else in the world. I have visited 50 countries and over 400 cities, and NONE gave me that sense of serenity that Bhutan has.

What is your favourite activity in Bhutan?

It is funny to say this, but one of my favourite parts of travelling to Bhutan is when the Drukair plane is landing at Paro International Airport. The way the pilots navigate the mountains and the view of the terrains below give me an adrenaline rush.

What are some of your most memorable experiences in Bhutan?

- Seeing the construction of Buddha Dordenma (from 2009 till its completion) during my 8 visits.

- Met former MD of National Housing Development Corporation and Election Commission, Dasho Uygen, and his beautiful family.

- Assisted in raising awareness about the needs of the young monks at Chusing Gonpa and raised funds to support their well-being.

- The opportunities to meet and learn from many learned Rinpoches.

- Attended Bhutan's National Day celebration on 17th Dec 2017 at Changlimithang Stadium. I was invited to dance with the officials.

- Ascending Tiger's Nest 5 times.

- The most important of all was meeting His Holiness, the 70th Je Khenpo, the Dorji Lopen, His Majesty the King of Bhutan, as well as the Prime Minister and a few of the cabinet ministers.

What are some qualities or traits that you admire about the Bhutanese?

I love the simplicity of the Bhutanese people, their devotion to Buddhism, filial piety and respect for the elderly people. Aside from that, I also admire their environmental awareness and their respect for the King, royal family, and His Holiness, the Chief Abbot. The Bhutanese people are very respectful and helpful to visitors, which is why I love visiting the kingdom.

Which are some of your favourite places in Bhutan?

Too many but below are three of my favourite locations:

Tiger's Nest is first on my list of favourite places. No two ascends are the same, and the magical feeling when you reach the top is beyond words!

Buddha Dordenma, the magnificent statue of the Buddha, tops all the statues I have paid homage to around the world.

Last but not least, **Phobjikha Valley** is another favourite to watch the black-necked cranes. Apart from watching the cranes, it is also an awesome place for mountain biking which I love tremendously.

What is your favourite Bhutanese food?

Has to be ema datshi (chilli cheese). It goes well with everything. I am vegetarian, and I find the vegetables in Bhutan to be very fresh and tasty whichever way it is prepared.

Robin Yap spent the last 42 years in the travel business. He has visited 50 countries and over 400 cities. He has repeatedly visited Bhutan more than any other country. He takes a personal interest in monasteries and temples. Outside of travel, he has served as a District Council in the Northwest District in Singapore over the past 15 years, focusing on promoting SkillsFuture training. He loves nature and sports. As an avid cyclist, he loves cycling in different countries and on different terrains; cycling in Bhutan is his newfound love.

How would you describe Bhutan to your friends?

I always tell my friends, if you haven't inhaled fresh air in your country, go to Bhutan. The mountains and Bhutan's negative carbon offers the cleanest air to clear our lungs! It is also a country of extreme beauty and I think it's comparable to Switzerland but with a lot more character in its architecture and calmness.

How many times have you been to Bhutan?

I have been to Bhutan 8 times and you can read about my visits on my blog https://bit.ly/TrulyBhutan.

Who is the most interesting person you've met in Bhutan so far?

It has to be His Majesty the King of Bhutan. I met him once in 2014 at Taj Tashi and at Khamsum Yulley Namgyal Chorten in 2018. I had the honour of having a 10 minutes audience with His Majesty and am super impressed by his knowledge of world events and Singapore. I have the highest respect for His Majesty for his devotion to the people of Bhutan.

Any other comments or thoughts?

I must have been a Bhutanese in my past life as I feel like I'm back home each time I arrive in Bhutan. Having been to 50 countries, only Bhutan gives me that homecoming feeling.

With the young monks in Chusing Gonpa

Enjoying cycling in Bhutan

My travel buddy and I enjoying ourselves in Phobjikha Valley

Baki Zainal

"Bhutan is a reset button or a recharge station for your mind, soul and body. It's like an Asian magical land that time has kind of forgotten."

When did you first set foot in Bhutan?

As a traveller, Bhutan has always been on my bucket list. The first time I set foot in this beautiful land was autumn of 2018.

What was your first impression of the country?

I don't know about other travellers, but no matter how much I researched Bhutan, nothing really prepared me for this beautiful country. My first impression was definitely the views as we were approaching Paro Airport. I can remember how majestic it was as the plane positioned itself between two cliffs. As we were landing, I could see all these traditional houses decorating the cliff. Bhutanese were in their traditional clothes, harvesting the land and just going on with their daily life. It all seemed like a scene that came to life from a movie set. It was just surreal. From that moment, I knew that this trip would be really special, and the best thing I could do was to leave all my expectations behind and get ready to be mesmerised by this new adventure.

What are some of your most memorable experiences in Bhutan?

Honestly, if I were to list them all, I would have to say it's the whole journey. However, 2 things happened that were just magical to me. The first would be the visit to Simply Bhutan. The locals showed us how they would pound the earth to build their houses, but what stood out to me was that as they were pounding, they were singing this nomadic-sounding song. It was about 4pm, and the snow caps in the background were turning into a nice warm golden colour. The song that they were singing was very hypnotising. So when they finished the demonstration, I asked them what the song was about, and they told us that it was not a song. It was a prayer. And the prayer was for all the souls of the ants, worms and everything on earth that had to sacrifice for us humans to have a roof above our heads. At that moment, I just felt a warm stream of tears roll down my cold cheeks. That was one of the most unselfish and beautiful things I had heard of in my whole life.

The other magical moment for me would be walking among the low clouds in Gangtey during sunset and seeing hundreds of black-necked cranes fly just above us. You might ask what is so special about seeing these birds. Well, first of all, according to the locals, it is very difficult to see them out in the wild, and on that cold day, I remember that we saw a few black dots far in the valley, and it was impossible to see them clearly in the flesh. But as we gave up hope, hundreds of them flew just above us, giving us a clear view of how majestic these beautiful birds were.

What are some qualities or traits that you admire about the Bhutanese?

I love how they appreciate life. They cherish and value every single moment in life. They celebrate everything around them. That sense of gratitude and being at peace with everything around them just makes me wonder what it is that we are chasing in our hectic life; what is happiness to us?

An avid traveller, Baki Zainal has been hosting various travel documentaries and TV shows across Asia for the past 16 years. Hailing from Malaysia, Baki is a household name and has been in the entertainment industry for the past 20 years. Of late, Baki has started producing his own TV shows. He is the face of a few international brands, including GoPro. Baki is tirelessly creating more content for his social media platform, @bakizainal.

The feeling of awe when the black-necked cranes were flying above us

How do you feel as a Muslim travelling to a predominantly Buddhist country?

As a Muslim, I love seeing and experiencing the many similarities we have. People might think that it was difficult for a Muslim boy like me to find food there, but it was not. Bhutan, being a predominantly Buddhist country, has so many vegetarian choices. I would say it's the best cuisine in Bhutan and you should try it. All the veggies are unintentionally grown organically. On top of that, everything is extra sweet and fresh.

Which is your favourite place in Bhutan?

I would have to say the Gangtey valley! Walking amongst the clouds and seeing the crazy colours as the sky changed was just superbly magical.

How would you describe your travel experience and journey in Bhutan?

Bhutan is a reset button or a recharge station for your mind, soul and body. It's like an Asian magical land that time has kind of forgotten.

Chilling at Ambient Cafe in Thimphu town

What advice do you have for people who are contemplating travelling to Bhutan?

Don't wait anymore. Just do it. It is not expensive. Honestly, it can be cheaper to travel to Bhutan than to Europe. It will be a journey that you will never ever forget.

What was the most interesting thing you learned about the Bhutanese culture?

The way they perceive life and how advanced their culture is compared to many so-called 'advanced' nations of the world. They are open-minded without losing their roots.

You can have a photo shoot anywhere in Bhutan

Write a review of Bhutan Travelog

We'd appreciate it if you could take some time to write us a book review on **www.bhutantravelog.com.**

We also aspire to feature all the inspiring wanderlust stories from travellers who have visited Bhutan.

Visit the website to share your photos and stories with the world.

facebook.com/bhutantravelog

@bhutantravelog

@bhutantravelog

Check out **www.bhutantravelog.com** for more Bhutan travel inspirations.

Bhutan in a Nutshell

1. **One of the safest countries in the world**

   Bhutan has effectively handled the COVID-19 pandemic. With just 37 doctors, 1,200 vaccination centres and less than 3,000 healthcare workers, 95% of its eligible population are fully vaccinated, as of July 2021.

2. **Top sustainable green destination**

   Green Destinations awarded Bhutan with the Earth Award in 2018 and Gold Award in 2019 for its sustainable and green initiatives, topping 100 sustainable destinations in the world.

3. **Birthplace of Gross National Happiness (GNH)**

   Upon Bhutan's proposal, the United Nations has adopted happiness as a development indicator. Since 2012, March 20 is celebrated as International Happiness Day.

4. **A country that doesn't have any traffic lights**

   You will not find a single traffic light in the entire country. Instead, you'll see traffic police controlling the traffic in the heart of the capital city, Thimphu.

5. **'High value, Low volume' sustainable tourism policy**

   Unlike other destinations, you will not suffer from overcrowding at tourist attractions. In fact, places are so quiet, you can take your time with a proper photoshoot.

6. **The only carbon negative country in the world**

   Today, Bhutan is the only carbon negative country in the world. It's no surprise that some say there's magic in the air.

7. **Home to the highest unclimbed mountain in the world**

   Since Bhutan prohibits mountaineering beyond 6,000 metres, Gangkar Puensum, standing at 7,570 metres above sea level, is the world's highest unclimbed mountain.

8. **Locals live in harmony with nature**

   The Bhutanese have the utmost respect for the natural environment including the forests, rocks, cliffs, lakes, rivers, water springs and mountains. They are deemed abodes of the local deities.

9. **Bhutan is one of the most peaceful places in the world**

   The Bhutanese take great pride living in Bhutan, a very peaceful and safe country. There are few crimes reported in the country, including in the major districts.

10. **Democracy in Bhutan is a gift from the throne**

    "We cannot leave such a small, vulnerable country in the hands of one person, who is chosen by birth and not by merit. Therefore, the Bhutanese must choose their own leader," said the fourth King, Jigme Singye Wangchuck.

11. A country blessed with compassionate and visionary monarchs

The Bhutanese have a deep love and respect for their king. The kings of Bhutan have always put the country before themselves. As such, the monarchs have constantly been a source of inspiration to the Bhutanese.

12. One of the top biodiversity hotspots in the world

You can find thriving populations of endangered animals in Bhutan due to their efforts in protection and conservation. Currently, there are five national parks, four wildlife sanctuaries and one nature reserve that covers 51.32% of the country's area.

13. The most hospitable people that you'll ever meet

The Bhutanese are incredibly kind, generous and warm people. They'll not hesitate to offer their help. You can rest assured that your safety and wellbeing are taken care of when you're in the country. Also, Bhutanese have common names. So, don't be surprised if you meet plenty of new friends named Ugyen, Sonam, Karma, Kinley or Pema.

14. Strong cultural identity and traditions

Bhutan is a country rich in cultural heritage. It has a lot to offer to travellers from abroad. The fabled kingdom boasts centuries-old architecture, sacred dances, significant Buddhist rituals, and highly devoted people.

15. Spectacular landscapes that are feasts for the eyes

The kingdom has an unspoiled natural environment, an extensive range of flora and fauna, spectacular Himalayan mountains, and an atmosphere that makes you want to visit again and again.

16. Healthy diet and lifestyle

If you're a health-conscious person, you can get relief knowing that Bhutanese food is healthy as most ingredients are grown organically within the country. In fact, the kingdom has an audacious goal to become the first wholly organic nation.

17. A very accessible tourist destination

Bhutan is definitely a remote country that's easily accessible if you want to travel off the beaten track to explore somewhere exclusive. There are direct flights from various Asian countries such as Bangkok, Singapore, India, Bangladesh and Nepal.

18. Bhutan is a country that will enrich you spiritually

In Bhutan, everything has a story, a meaning, or a lesson. Many people travel to Bhutan to seek inner peace and escape from the hustle and bustle of city life. It's the perfect location to contemplate the deeper meanings of life. But, one can only feel its true essence and magic by being physically there to experience it.

Glossary

Ara
Rice wine.

Atsara
Jesters or clowns who entertain the crowd during a tshechu.

Bangchu
Circular bamboo container with a lid.

Bodhisattva
Enlightened beings in Mahayana Buddhism.

Bon
Religion with shamanistic and animist practices that predate Buddhism in the Himalayan region.

Bonpo
Bon priests.

Brokpas
Inhabitants of the valleys of Merak and Sakteng in eastern Bhutan.

Bumpa
Sacred vessel.

Bukhari
Traditional wood-burning stove.

Chhu
River or water.

Choesi
Dual system of governance.

Choesum
An elaborately decorated shrine room with an altar that also serves as a guest room.

Chorten
Religious structure, also known as stupa, usually containing sacred relics.

Chugo
A hard cheese made from yak's milk.

Dapa
Lustrous wooden bowl or cup.

Dasho
An honorary title conferred by the king.

Desi
Title given to the temporal ruler of Bhutan from 1851 to 1905.

Desuung
Guardians of Peace.

Doma
Areca nut and slaked lime wrapped in betel leaf.

Dorje
Thunderbolt.

Dratshang
Commision for the Monastic Affairs in Bhutan.

Driglam Namzha
Official code of etiquette and dress code in Bhutan.

Druk
Thunder Dragon.

Druk Gyalpo
Formal title held by the ruler of Bhutan, the King of Bhutan.

Drukpa
People from Bhutan.

Druk Yul
Land of the Thunder Dragon, the name for
Bhutan in Dzongkha.

Drukpa Kargyupa
The sect of Buddhism that is the official
state religion of Bhutan.

Drukpa Kuenley
Saint of the Drukpa Kagyu school, who
spread his unorthodox teachings.

Duar
Doorway or gate, which refers to the
traditional entrances to Bhutan from the
Bengal and Assam plains of India.

Dungpa
Administrator of a sub-district.

Dzong
Ancient fortress in Bhutan that usually
houses administrative offices as well as the
monastic body.

Dzongda
Administrative head of a district.

Dzongkha
The official language of Bhutan (literally,
language spoken in the dzong).

Dzongkhag
District.

Ema datsi
Dish of chillies cooked with cheese.

Ezay
A chutney or relish made with chillies.

Gewog
A county consisting of a block of villages.

Gho
Men's traditional dress; a knee-length robe
secured with a handwoven belt.

Goen Hogay
Cucumber salad.

Goenkhang
Inner sanctum.

Gomchen
Lay monk or ascetic.

Gompa
Monastery.

Gyalsung
National service.

Guru Padmasambhava
The Indian saint who brought Buddhism to
Bhutan in the eighth century; also popularly
known as Guru Rinpoche.

Je Khenpo
Chief Abbot of Bhutan, and official head of
the Drukpa Kagyu school.

Jigme Dorji Wangchuck
Third King of Bhutan.

Jigme Khesar Namgyel Wangchuck
Fifth King of Bhutan.

Jigme Namgyel
Tongsa Penlop and fiftieth desi of Bhutan;
father of the first King.

Jigme Singye Wangchuck
Fourth King of Bhutan.

Jigme Wangchuck
Second King of Bhutan.

Kabney

Ceremonial scarf worn by men.

Karma
The universal law of cause and effect.

Kasho
Royal decree.

Kera
Woven belt.

Kewa datshi
Potato cheese.

Khuru
A game of darts.

Kira
Women's traditional dress, an ankle-length dress held together by a brooch.

Koma
Brooches to fasten the women's *kira* at the shoulder.

Kishuthara
An elaborate and intricately woven Bhutanese textile.

La
Mountain pass.

Lam Neten
Head abbot of a district.

Lama
Buddhist priest who is a religious master.

Layaps
People from Laya in the northern highlands of Bhutan.

Lhakhang
Buddhist temple.

Lhotsampa
Persons of Nepali origin who are settled in Bhutan.

Mani wall
Stone walls carved with the Buddhist mantra: *Om mani padme hum.*

Ney
Sacred site.

Ngultrum
Bhutanese currency (BTN).

Penlop
Historic title given to governors of the three big dzongs of Paro, Trongsa and Daga.

Rachu
Women's ceremonial scarf; draped over the left shoulder.

Rinpoche
The 'precious one'; reincarnated lama.

Sharchopkha
The language spoken in eastern Bhutan.

Songtsen Gampo
King of Tibet in the seventh century who built the first Buddhist temples in Bhutan.

Samsara
The continuous cycle of life, death and reincarnation.

Shamu Datshi
Mushroom cheese.

Stupa
A dome-shaped Buddhist shrine.

Suja
Butter tea.

Takin (Budorcas taxicolor)
National animal of Bhutan, scientifically

classified as a goat-antelope, found in the highlands of Bhutan.

Terma
Hidden treasure.

Terton
Treasure revealer.

Thangka
Buddhist scroll painting.

Thongdrel
Large painted or embroidered silk banners hung from the wall of a dzong or monastery on important religious occasions.

Trulku
Reincarnated master; spiritual head of a monastery.

Tsatsa
Miniature cylindrical-shaped stupas made from clay and sometimes mixed with ashes of the deceased.

Tshachu
Hot spring.

Tsatsi Buram
Sweet made from sugarcane.

Tshechu
Religious festival held in honour of Guru Padmasambhava.

Tsho
Lake.

Tshogdu
National Assembly of Bhutan.

Ugyen Wangchuck
First King of Bhutan.

Utse
Central tower of a dzong.

Wonju
Women's long-sleeved blouse, worn under the kira.

Yathra
Colourful woollen textile woven in the Bumthang district of Bhutan.

Zaw
Roasted rice.

Zorig Chusum
The thirteen traditional arts and crafts of Bhutan.

Ashley Chen

Ashley is an avid traveller who enjoys learning about the different creeds and cultures. Aside from her passion for writing and photography, she is a curious wanderer with a philosophical streak, constantly seeking to discover more about herself and the world around her.

She contributes to the Bhutanese society by sharing her expertise in the non-profit sphere and acts as an international consultant to the Gyalyum Charitable Trust in Bhutan. She is also the editor of *Daily Bhutan*, an independent news outlet that brings the latest news, educational features and inspiring stories from Bhutan to a global audience.

When in Bhutan, Ashley fits seamlessly into the Bhutanese society, often mistaken as a local wherever she goes. Believing that each individual is unique and possesses different perspectives, she appreciates deep and meaningful conversations with the people she encounters.

Joni Herison

Joni has been involved in Bhutan's tourism industry for more than a decade. He is the Managing Director of Druk Asia, one of the pioneering Bhutan tour operators outside of Bhutan. He has a deep love for the kingdom and has played a pivotal role in connecting Bhutan with travellers from all over the world. Joni is a cherished friend of the kingdom and has built an excellent rapport with the Bhutanese community.

He has visited Bhutan 31 times in the past decade. Each of his visits to the kingdom rejuvenated his spirits and spurred him to continue promoting Bhutan as a travel destination. A bibliophile with a cheerful disposition, Joni can always be found with a cup of coffee and a self-enrichment book at hand.

Indonesian by birth and Bhutanese by heart, Joni has put down roots in Singapore with his lovely wife, Eileen, and three adorable children.

Notes

Notes

Notes